DOMINICAN REPUBLIC

Michael Grosberg, Trent Holden

Meet our writers

Michael Grosberg

linkedin.com/in/michael-grosberg-9912858

Michael has worked over 75 Lonely Planet guidebooks, including four previous editions of the Lonely Planet *Dominican Republic* book and he's the co-founder of travel start-up LikeLocal (likelocal.io). His favorite experience is diving and snorkeling in the waters off Las Terrenas (p129) and hiking with his two young daughters.

Trent Holden

@hombreholden

A writer for Lonely Planet for 15 years, Trent's covered destinations across South America, Asia, Africa, Australia and Europe.

MAREMAGNUM/GETTY IMAGES

Previous spread Cascada El Limón (p116)

ATLANTIDE PHOTOTRAVEL/GETTY IMAGES

0
0
100 km
50 miles
ATLANTIC OCEAN
Cabrera
Bahía Escocesa
Península de Samaná 108
Nagua
Las Terrenas
Las Galeras
Península de Samaná
Samaná
Sabana de la Mar
Miches
Playa Limón
Monte Plata
Hato Mayor
El Seibo
El Puerto
Cabarete 5½ hrs
Bávaro
Barahona 3½ hrs
Santo Domingo 44
Higüey
Bávaro 2¾ hrs
San Pedro de Macorís
Punta Cana & the Southeast 78
Punta Cana
SANTO DOMINGO
Boca Chica
Juan Dolio
La Romana
Bayahibe
Boca de Yuma
Isla Catalina
Isla Saona
CARIBBEAN SEA

Find your own idyllic palm-fringed beach paradise. Cool off at the base of hidden waterfalls. Slide or raft your way down rocky rapids. Hike to the Caribbean's highest peak. Plunge underneath aquamarine waters. Lose yourself dancing in a raucous nightclub or Carnival. Spot wildlife on the move amid stunning landscapes. Get in the know about culture and history. Tour and taste your way through factory workshops. Take in end-of-the-road panoramic beach views.

This is the Dominican Republic.

TURN THE PAGE AND START PLANNING YOUR NEXT BEST TRIP →

Monte Cristi
La Isabela
Puerto Plata
Cofresí
Punta Rucia
Cabarete
Fort Liberté
Santiago 1½ hrs
Las Terrenas 4hrs
Navarette
Dajabón
Mao
North Coast 132
Santiago
Moca
Sabaneta
HAITI
Salcedo
Restauración
Santo Domingo 2-3hrs
San Francisco de Macorís
Central Highlands 162
La Vega
Hinche
Jarabacoa
Cotuí
El Río
Bonao
Mirebalais
San Juan de la Maguana
Constanza
Elías Piña
DOMINICAN REPUBLIC
San José de Ocoa
Jimaní
Neiba
Lago Enriquillo
San Cristóbal
Ázua
Baní
Barahona
The Southwest 200
Pedernales
Península de Pedernales
Laguna Oviedo
Isla Beata
Isla Alto Velo

Catamaran, Playa El Cortecito (p97)

Contents

LUCAS VALLECILLOS/ALAMY

Above Musicians, Santo Domingo

WET & WILD

From the Caribbean's only white-water raftable river to thrilling canyoning adventures and deep plunge pools at the foot of jungle-concealed waterfalls, the Dominican Republic might have the most concentrated freshwater adventures around. Some are refreshing, but relatively placid, while others may push past your comfort level, but all will be a highlight of your trip.

Left Cascada El Limón (p116) **Right** White-water rafting on Río Yaque (p169) **Below** Salto de la Jalda

→ BASE YOURSELF

The North Coast beach town of Cabarete and the mountain town of Jarabacoa are the best bases from which to enjoy a variety of adrenaline-fueled activities.

▶ Cabarete p138

▶ Jarabacoa p168

DANITA DELIMONT/ALAMY

WHAT TO PACK

Besides high SPF sunscreen, a hat, sunglasses and bug spray, pack river shoes, a dry bag, rash guard and travel beach towel to help you stay safe and dry off during and after your water adventures.

FROM LEFT: JON ARNOLD IMAGES LTD/ALAMY, ONAPALMTREE/SHUTTERSTOCK

↑ SECLUDED FALLS

Little-visited Salto de la Jalda, at 120m, is the highest-drop waterfall in the country and is only accessible by a 14km round-trip hike.

Best Freshwater Experiences

▶ **Dive into an amazing natural waterpark at 27 Waterfalls of Damajagua.** (p146)

▶ **Cool off after your hike in Cascada El Limón pool outside Las Terrenas.** (p116)

▶ **Get your adrenaline pumping by rafting the Río Yaque's white water.** (p169)

▶ **Plunge into a cenote's turquoise waters surrounded by mangroves.** (p105)

▶ **Go canyoning, a water-based version of parkour, through a river-filled slot canyon.** (p169)

MADE IN THE DR

More than simply the lifeblood of the economy, iconic Dominican commodities and products, like chocolate, coffee, cigars, Larimar jewelry and rum, are integral ingredients of Dominican society and life. From small-scale to industrial-sized operations, farms, factories and workshops open their sweet-smelling, intoxicating doors to curious visitors.

FRANCISCO RODRIGUEZ HERNA/SHUTTERSTOCK

Left Roasted coffee beans **Right** Bottle of rum produced in the Dominican Republic **Below** Larimar stones

→ FANCY A TIPPLE?

The Dominican Republic is the world's second-largest exporter of rum, after the United States.

HOMEGROWN CROP

Some of the world's finest cigars contain tobacco grown on the hillsides around the town of Moca; coffee and cocoa are also produced here.

▶ p188

FROM LEFT: JIMMYVILLALTA/GETTY IMAGES, MARVIN DEL CID/GETTY IMAGES

↑ EXCLUSIVE TO THE DR

The rare blue mineral Larimar was discovered in 1974 on a beach in the province of Barahona.

▶ p220

Best Behind the Scenes

- **Satisfy your sweet tooth on the Sendero del Cacao.** (p193)
- **Learn how stogies are made by hand at a factory outside the city of Santiago.** (p188)
- **Get to know how Larimar, the Dominican Republic's most unique precious stone, is mined and processed.** (p220)
- **Tour a coffee plantation and bean processing factory to see how your cup of Joe is made.** (p194)
- **Drink your fill of rum at the plant of one of the best-known brands.** (p149)

A BEACH FOR EVERYBODY

From palm-backed isolated oases to sandy shores as packed as a rush hour subway car, the country's Atlantic and Caribbean coastlines can satisfy every taste and demand. The DR is blessed with year-round warm temperatures and waters of every hue, so bring a boatload of suntan lotion, a good book or two, and an appetite for freshly grilled seafood served alfresco.

Left Resort beach lounges, Punta Cana **Right** Beachfront bar, Sosúa **Below** Bahía de las Águilas (p205)

→ DINING BEACHSIDE

Few experiences are more quintessentially Dominican than milking a couple of Presidente *grandes* (beers) and enjoying a grilled seafood meal at a plastic table on a beach.

▸ p94

ERIC JAMES/ALAMY

STAY SAFE

Before swimming in the ocean without lifeguards present, ask locals for advice on rip tides and currents.

FROM LEFT: KELLYSHUTSTOC/SHUTTERSTOCK, PHOTOFXS68/GETTY IMAGES

↑ SECLUDED BEACHES

Private, isolated beach paradises are hard to come by in the DR. However, island-hopping around the Bahía de las Águilas in the southwest is your best bet.

▸ p205

Best Beaches

- **Make the journey to far-flung, hard-to-get-to Bahía de las Águilas, where cacti hug the cliffs over the beach.** (p205)
- **Wander Playa Rincón's 3km of tropical paradise with a nearby stream to wash off the salt water.** (p123)
- **Enjoy the perfect Caribbean holiday at one of Punta Cana's resorts.** (p100)
- **Make a day of it at one of the golden stretches in Río San Juan's half-moon cove.** (p152)
- **Day drink and dine on Sosúa's town beach.** (p144)

The DR has set aside over 10% of its land as national parks and scientific reserves.

Bats eat as many as 2000 mosquitoes a night.

There are over 5600 species of plants on the island.

PARKS & RECREATION

Blessed with lush valleys, mangrove lagoons, remote wind-swept desert landscapes and a mountain range so big that it casts a rain shadow that contributes to the aridity of the southwest, the DR has worked to protect its biological diversity through the creation of an extensive national park system and scientific preserves.

Left Parque Nacional Los Haitises (p84) **Right** Manatee **Below** Royal terns

→ MANATEES

Santuario de Mamíferos Marinos Estero Hondo (near Punta Rucia) and Parque Nacional Monte Cristi are two of the better places to try to spot manatees, either in a boat, from a watchtower or kayaking coastal lagoons and mangroves.

WRANGEL/GETTY IMAGES

MINI MAMMALS

Besides a number of bat species, only two native land mammal species remain: the hutia, a tree climbing rodent, and the endemic solenodon, an insectivore resembling a giant shrew.

FROM LEFT: VÍCTOR GÓMEZ/ALAMY, PATRICK MESSIER/SHUTTERSTOCK

↑ TWITCHING HIGHLIGHTS

More than 300 bird species, including 33 endemic species, have been recorded on the island.

Best Wildlife-Spotting

- **Spy humpbacks in Bahía de Samaná.** (p118)
- **Look out for crocodiles and iguanas (and flamingos and egrets December to April) in Lago Enriquillo.** (p211)
- **Spot flamingos, ibis, storks and spoonbills, not to mention egg-laying turtles and iguanas, at Laguna Oviedo.** (p208)
- **Kayak Parque Nacional Los Haitises for birds, boas, manatees and turtles.** (p84)
- **Take in truly stunning views from the edge of Hoyo de Pelempito.** (p219)

IAN DAGNALL COMMERCIAL COLLECTION/GETTY IMAGES

- Coffee is typically served black with lots of sugar.
- Many restaurants are closed between lunch and dinner.
- Coconut juice from a *cocotero* (street vendor) costs around RD$40 to RD$50.

TAKE A **BITE**

Whether you're mellowing out with an espresso at a downtown cafe or feasting on a whole grilled fish served up on a beach, one of the DR's common denominators – regardless of region, setting or status – is an unabashed joy in gathering family and friends for a healthy heaping of food and drink.

Best Meals

- **Don't settle for the *plato del día* in Santo Domingo when you can try haute cuisine with a Dominican twist on the balcony of a colonial-era building.** (p75)
- **Come for the views as much as the seafood at a waterfront restaurant in Boca de Yuma.** (p95)
- **Pull up a chair at a Playa Sosúa shack for a burger, *tostones* (smashed, fried plantains) and beer.** (p144)

NATURAL HIGHS

Cloud-covered peaks and mountainous, rugged terrain aren't the first images that usually come to mind when dreaming of Caribbean island hideaways. Yet, four of the five highest peaks in the Caribbean rise above the fertile lowlands around Santiago, so there's no shortage of pretty pastoral panoramas more than worth the blisters.

Best Highs

- **Overnight it to Pico Duarte, the highest peak in the Caribbean.** (p174)
- **Trek up Mogote, a challenging, steep hike near Jarabacoa.** (p171)
- **Go on a hike around jungle-clad terrain from Tubagua Plantation outside Puerto Plata.** (p154)
- **Cool off in the Caribbean's highest-altitude town of Constanza.** (p173)

FROM LEFT: AUTHORSIMAGE/ALAMY, MATYAS REHAK/ALAMY

← ON THE RISE

The summit of Pico Duarte is 3098m and rising: the Caribbean plate moves 1cm to 2cm per year, elevating Hispaniola around 5cm every 100 years.

▶ p174

★ THE DR'S BREADBASKET

Eighty percent of produce and 75% of flowers are grown around the high valley of Constanza, the fertile 'breadbasket' of the DR.

▶ p173

Above Pico Duarte landscape
Left Farm near Constanza
Far left Beachfront restaurant, Sosúa

THE PARTY NEVER STOPS

From impromptu neighborhood block parties gathering around the local *colmado* (corner store), swanky hotel nightclubs or local fiestas, Dominicans love to drink, socialize and get down. Wherever you are in the country, the central square is a likely nighttime gathering place. The cities of Santo Domingo and Santiago are dancing highlights. And Carnival is the biggest blowout of the year.

ORIOLE GIN/SHUTTERSTOCK

Left Dancers, Grupo Bonyé (p63)
Right Carnival parade, Punta Cana
Below Coco Bongo, Punta Cana

→ CARNIVAL

The largest and most traditional Carnivals outside Santo Domingo are celebrated in La Vega, Santiago, Monte Cristí and Cabral.

▶ p182

ATMOSPHERIC DRINKS

Many of Santo Domingo's and Santiago's best bars and clubs are found in their architecturally beautiful and walkable historic downtowns.

▶ Santo Domingo p62
▶ Santiago p178

FROM LEFT: JIMMY VILLALTA/VWPICS/ALAMY; PHOTOPIXEL/SHUTTERSTOCK

↑ TICKETS, PLEASE

Some of the biggest international artists perform in several large venues in the Punta Cana area, including Hard Rock Hotel & Casino and Coco Bongo.

▶ p100

Best Nights Out

▶ **Let loose with *capitaleños* at a dance party in the ruins of a colonial monastery on Sunday nights.** (p63)

▶ **Hit Santo Domingo's Av Rómulo Betancourt for good drinks, great views and live music.** (p65)

▶ **Blow things out at La Vega's Carnival, where the entire city turns out for raucous fun.** (p180)

▶ **Dance merengue in Santiago, where the music and moves were created.** (p186)

ARTS & CULTURE

The heart of the Spanish colonial enterprise in the DR is chockablock with museums, monuments and sights to transport you back in time. But it's not only Santo Domingo's Zona Colonial: Santiago and Puerto Plata have their own institutions marking bygone eras and the Taíno people have left traces of their presence carved onto cave walls.

FEDERICO PARRA/GETTY IMAGES

Left Historic building, Puerto Plata **Right** Baseball spectators, Santo Domingo **Below** Taíno pictographs, Reserva Antropológica Cuevas del Pomier (p224)

→ PLAY BALL

One good window into Dominicans' cultural passions – food, drink, music, dance and, of course, sports – can be had by attending a baseball game.

▸ p58

DAY-TRIPPING

Some do a whistle-stop tour of Santo Domingo on an extremely long day trip from Punta Cana. This city's historical institutions alone call for a much longer visit.

FROM LEFT: ROBERTHARDING/ALAMY VW PICS/GETTY IMAGES

↑ TAÍNO TRACES

Find a cave anywhere throughout the DR and you're likely to find Taíno pictographs painted on its walls.

▸ p86

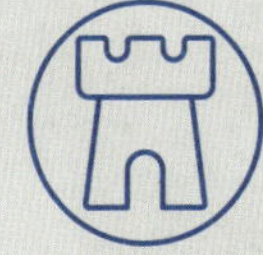

Best Back in Time

- **Follow in the footsteps of conquistadors along Santo Domingo's cobblestone streets.** (p50)
- **Trace the foundations of a settlement established by Columbus.** (p156)
- **View some of the DR's most well-known artists at Santiago's Centro León.** (p179)
- **Walk past Puerto Plata's Victorian-era mansions to the ramparts of a fortress.** (p148)
- **Marvel at the intricacy of ancient cave paintings at Cueva de las Maravillas.** (p87)

OCEAN SPORTS

The Dominican Republic's vast and varied coastal geography caters to extreme sports as well as subaquatic adventures in both its Atlantic and Caribbean waters. If it involves standing on a board, the DR's got it in spades, and while its reputation as a diving destination might not compare to other Caribbean islands, there are more than enough sites – from wrecks to caves and shark-spotting – to design a trip around.

Left Kitesurfers, Kite Beach (p139)
Right Surf shack, Cabarete
Below Surf school student

→ BEST BASES

Cabarete and Sosúa on the North Coast, Bayahibe in the southeast and Las Terrenas on the Península de Samaná are the best bases to take advantage of most activities.

MARY BARATTO/SHUTTERSTOCK

BOOK YOUR SPOT

Learning to kitesurf can be a time-intensive and expensive endeavor; if that's what brings you to the DR, it's best to organize your trip around this.

▸ p139

FROM LEFT: MARY BARATTO/SHUTTERSTOCK, EVGENIYQW/SHUTTERSTOCK

↑ LOW-KEY WAVES

Playa Buen Hombre, 124km west of Puerto Plata on the way to the Haitian border, is a charming, low-key, under-the-radar spot for kitesurfing and surfing.

▸ p140

Best Wind & Waves

- **Skim across the waves at high speeds in Cabarete and Buen Hombre.** (p139)
- **Boat out to reefs around Playa Frontón for some of the best snorkeling and diving.** (p129)
- **Explore a spring water–fed sinkhole with several underwater caverns near the town of Río San Juan.** (p152)
- **Catch a wave surfing around Playa Encuentro's breaks just west of Cabarete.** (p143)
- **Dive Sosúa's crystal-clear waters, reefs, walls and canyons.** (p144)

July to August is high season for accommodations; book ahead.

Hot, Hot, Hot

City sightseeing and the southwest especially can be uncomfortably hot and humid; coastal areas preferred. Good deals abound.

↖ Jazz Fest

Cabarete's Jazz Festival kicks off for three days toward the end of June.

↓ Seaweed Season

A natural phenomenon, the annual infestation of sargasso seaweed washes ashore on the country's eastern beaches from July through September.

JUNE

Average daytime max: 32°C (90°F)
Days of rainfall: 12

JULY

Dominican Republic in SUMMER

FROM LEFT: GEORGIAFLASH/ALAMY, SBORISOV/GETTY IMAGES, JUDYDILLON/GETTY IMAGES, GREGORYGOMEZ4/SHUTTERSTOCK, POLA DAMONTE/GETTY IMAGES

Good, Strong Winds

The most consistent windy conditions along the northern Dominican coasts makes it prime time for kitesurfing.

▶ p138

↑ Dance Time

Santo Domingo's annual merengue festival heats up the city in the last week of July.

▶ p74

← Hatching Time

It's turtle-nesting season for several species in the Bahía de las Águilas and Laguna Oviedo.

Average daytime max: 32°C (90°F)
Days of rainfall: 14

AUGUST

Average daytime max: 32.5°C (91°F)
Days of rainfall: 14

Be flexible if you're hoping to go hiking or mountain-biking in the mountains; rains can put things on hold for days at a time.

Packing Notes

Umbrella and raincoat for rain showers, and light everything for humidity.

Hurricane season runs from June to December (impacting the east), but September and October are typically the most vulnerable to big storms.

↘ Rebate Time

During the 'low' tourism season, you can find heavily discounted rooms, and some properties in resort areas close in October.

↖ World's Best

Cabarete hosts the Master of the Ocean competition for kitesurfing and other water sports the third weekend in September.

SEPTEMBER

Average daytime max: 33°C (92°F)
Days of rainfall: 7

OCTOBER

Dominican Republic in AUTUMN

FROM LEFT: LAGENTE.DO/SHUTTERSTOCK, YAKOV OSKANOV/SHUTTERSTOCK, EVGENIYQW/SHUTTERSTOCK, FELIX LEON/GETTY IMAGES, VALENTIN VALKOV/SHUTTERSTOCK

Starting Surf

Mellow waves along the North Coast makes this a good time for beginner surfers; not for experts.

▶ p142

Baseball Begins

The boys of winter get into full swing in November. Six teams in five cities (Santo Domingo has two) play several games a week through January.

▶ p58

Average daytime max: 32.5°C (91°F)
Days of rainfall: 11

Rainfall is heavier, nearly double, on the North Coast than on the southeast, where you can expect nearly as much sun.

Packing Notes

Dry bag for rainy days and boat rides, and river shoes for water-based adventures.

Hotel and flight prices rise through December and January, especially between Christmas and New Years, as Americans and Canadians begin their yearly exodus. Early December can be ideal.

↘ Whale-Watching

The North American winter coincides with the start of whale-watching season in the Bahía de Samaná.

▸ p118

← Pink Flamingos

Migratory patterns mean Laguna Oviedo's flamingo population peaks from December to March; there's no shortage of other birdlife to spot.

▸ p208

DECEMBER

Average daytime max: 28°C (83°F)
Days of rainfall: 7

JANUARY

Dominican Republic in WINTER

↓ Peak Trekking

Dry, clear skies make this prime time to climb Pico Duarte.

▶ p174

← Independence Holiday

February 27, 1844, the day the DR regained its independence from Haiti, is marked with raucous street celebrations and military parades.

← Carnival

Every Sunday in February is a fiesta in the lead-up to the biggest bash in the country at the end of the month.

▶ p182

FEBRUARY

Average daytime max: 28°C (83°F)
Days of rainfall: 7

Average daytime max: 28°C (83°F)
Days of rainfall: 4

Demand for accommodations peaks between mid-December through February. View tours and overnight adventures in advance at lonelyplanet.com

Packing Notes

One dressy nighttime outfit for resorts and warm layers for the mountainous interior.

North American spring breakers, both families and college students alike, flock to the country's beaches between mid-March and mid-April.

↘ March Madness

Semana Santa (Holy Week), the week before Easter, businesses close, Dominicans flock to beaches, and reservations are vital. Water sports are mostly prohibited and demand for accommodations peaks.

↖ Blooming Flora

April is a good time to visit Laguna Oviedo and the southwest; from March to June cactus flowers bloom in the desert.

▸ p208

MARCH

APRIL

Average daytime max: 27.5°C (82°F)
Days of rainfall: 11

Dominican Republic in SPRING

FROM LEFT: TITA S/SHUTTERSTOCK, JOHN MITCHELL/ALAMY, NICK HANNA/ALAMY, PHOTOPIXEL/SHUTTERSTOCK, VIKTOR_LA/SHUTTERSTOCK

↘ Head to the Highlands

Great season to head to the Cordillera region around Jarabacoa for hiking, mountain-biking and white-water rafting.

▶ p168

↗ Wind Sports

Winds and waves on the North Coast are strongest this time of year, attracting surfers and kitesurfers to the area's beaches.

▶ p138

Average daytime max: 28°C (83°F)
Days of rainfall: 11

MAY

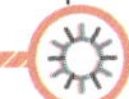

Average daytime max: 29°C (84°F)
Days of rainfall: 13

Outside coastal areas and May, especially, you can find reduced flights and hotel costs and overall great value.

Packing Notes

Warm clothes if heading to the highlands. SPF 50 or higher sunscreen always.

SANTO DOMINGO & THE EAST COAST

Trip Builder

ALL-INCLUSIVE RESORTS AND A HISTORICALLY SIGNIFICANT CAPITAL

People flock to the resorts around Punta Cana, the buffet and pool bar capital of the DR, but other waterborne adventures, waterfront towns and culinary options abound. The country's culture-filled capital is a lively cosmopolitan destination in and of itself.

Trip Notes

Hub towns Santo Domingo, Punta Cana, Bayahibe

How long Allow one week

Getting around The majority of travelers fly directly to Punta Cana's airport; however, Santo Domingo's airport is an equally viable option. Comfortable buses connect the major hubs. Ubers and taxis are expensive options. Renting a car provides the most flexibility.

Tips If you can hold off past the winter holidays, January and February offer the same sun and sand but a whole lot less people.

FROM TOP LEFT: WATERFRAME/ALAMY, MAYAKOVA/SHUTTERSTOCK, ORIOLE GIN/SHUTTERSTOCK

Zona Colonial
Explore this Santo Domingo neighborhood for many of the oldest colonial-era buildings and original treasures in the Americas, along with some of the region's best museums.
3hr from Punta Cana

0 50 km
0 25 miles

Sabana de la Mar

Navigate mangrove-infested forests on a tranquil kayak excursion through Parque Nacional Los Haitises.

2½ hr from Punta Cana

Punta Cana

Soak in the sun on the area's beaches; dive into freshwater lagoons and enjoy some of the DR's best restaurants.

1hr from Bayahibe

Boca de Yuma

Take a day trip to this quiet seaside promontory for seafood with views. Just west of town is a national park with a stalagmite-filled cave.

1¼ hr from Punta Cana

Cueva de las Maravillas

Plunge into an illuminated underworld at this massive underground museum. Nearby, beachfront bars and restaurants beckon.

1hr from Punta Cana

Bayahibe

Dive into aquamarine waters for snorkeling and diving adventures right outside your front door. Cocktails and fish taste better from a waterfront restaurant.

1hr from Punta Cana

Samaná
Sabana de la Mar
Miches
Playa Limón
Nisibón
Cordillera Oriental
Pedro Sánchez
El Seibo
Hato Mayor
Bávaro
Higüey
Punta Cana
Ramón Santana
Quisqueya
San Pedro de Macorís
La Romana
San Rafael del Yuma
Boca de Yuma
Bayahibe
Isla Catalina
Parque Nacional Cotubanamá
Isla Saona
Parque Nacional del Este

PENÍNSULA DE SAMANÁ
Trip Builder

TAKE YOUR PICK OF MUST-SEES AND HIDDEN GEMS

Find your happy place on trips to sublime beaches, jungle-clad waterfalls, rural valleys and oh-so-slow seaside villages. Wind-whipped waves, coral for snorkeling and diving, and wildlife are never far away.

Trip Notes

Hub towns Las Terrenas, Las Galeras, Samaná

How long Allow 10 days

Getting around *Guaguas* (local buses) and taxis are available. Rental vehicles, from motorcycles to ATVs, are popular.

Tips If possible, fly directly into Aeropuerto Internacional El Catey, the closest airport to the peninsula. Otherwise, improved highways mean manageable drives or buses from elsewhere. Try to time your visit with whale-watching season.

Las Terrenas
Enjoy a smorgasbord of beaches and culinary diversity, plus snorkeling, kitesurfing and day trips to out-of-the-way rural and seaside spots.
2½ hr from Santo Domingo

El Portillo
Las Terrenas

El Limón
Navigate the rugged and wet mountain scenery of Samaná's interior on a trip to a 52m-high waterfall, where you can cool off before the trek back to the village.
25min from Las Terrenas

Los Puentes
La Guazara
Los Robalos

Bahía de Samaná

Playa Rincón

Laze away the day on one of the peninsula's most gorgeous sun-toasted, sandy beaches with a freshwater dip and beachside feast.

30min from Las Galeras

Playa El Valle

Wake up in a jungle tree house near this relatively isolated and beautiful beach. The surrounding rural area offers a slow pace of life, with forested walks and horseback rides.

25min from Samaná

NORTH ATLANTIC OCEAN

El Limón

Monumento Natural Salto El Limón

El Valle

Las Galeras

Las Galeras

Let go of your worries while lounging, snorkeling and diving at isolated beaches. The end-of-the-road village offers an abundance of rural walks and seafront dining.

1½ hr from Las Terrenas

Arroyo Barril

Samaná

Cayo La Farola

Cayo Levantado

Samaná

Come mid-January to mid-March when humpback whales migrate to the Bahía de Samaná and whale-watching tours are in full steam.

40min from Las Galeras

0 10 km
0 5 miles

NORTH COAST
Trip Builder

TAKE YOUR PICK OF MUST-SEES AND HIDDEN GEMS

Discover bustling coastal towns, out-of-the-way beachside villages and a seaside regional capital with streets lined with Victorian-era architecture. Expect gorgeous vistas, top-flight surf and wind sports, and some of the country's best waterfall-based adventures.

Trip Notes

Hub towns Puerto Plata, Sosúa, Cabarete, Río San Juan

How long Allow 10 days

Getting around Rent a 4WD or catch a *guagua* between towns. Walk or motorcycle when based in one spot.

Tips Aeropuerto Internacional Gregorio Luperón in Puerto Plata is within two hours' driving distance of almost everywhere on the North Coast. Winds pick up from December to March.

FROM TOP LEFT: DMITRY CHULOV/SHUTTERSTOCK, STEFFEN ENGESSER/SHUTTERSTOCK, HEMIS.FR RM/GETTY IMAGES, MATYAS REHAK/ALAMY, YAVIMR/SHUTTERSTOCK

Puerto Plata
Snap photos of romantically decaying Victorian-era colonial buildings and get the lowdown on Dominican rum, chocolate and cigars.
1½hr from Santiago

Sosúa
Grab a snorkel or suit up with gear to go diving at a nearby offshore site. Wash down your meal with drinks at a beachside shack on Playa Sosúa.
40min from Puerto Plata

Cabarete
Fill your days with surfing, kitesurfing and canyoning. In the evenings, dig your toes in the sand and feast on seafood at a beachside restaurant.
15min from Sosúa

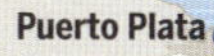

Damajagua
Wade through clear pools, swim inside narrow, smooth-walled canyons, and climb rocks, ropes and ladders through some of the 27 roaring falls.
30min from Puerto Plata

Río San Juan
Seek tranquility in a typical small-town Dominican atmosphere, with some of the country's most stunning beaches, including Playa Grande nearby.
1hr from Cabarete

CENTRAL HIGHLANDS
Trip Builder

TAKE YOUR PICK OF MUST-SEES AND HIDDEN GEMS

Head inland to experience a lesser-known side of the country, where you can climb high peaks, go on freshwater adrenaline-fueled activities and even huddle in a sweater at night. Down below in the plains of the Valle del Cibao, life revolves around Santiago, where merengue, rum and cigars can be appreciated.

Trip Notes

Hub towns Jarabacoa, Constanza, Santiago

How long Allow five days

Getting around Fly into Santiago's Aeropuerto Internacional del Cibao; rent a 4WD to explore countryside outside Constanza.

Tips Santiago's and La Vega's Carnival celebrations are two of the country's finest.

Parque Nacional Armando Bermúdez
Summit the roof of the Caribbean and mountain bike your way through scenic forests in one of the DR's most biodiverse national parks.
1hr from Jarabacoa

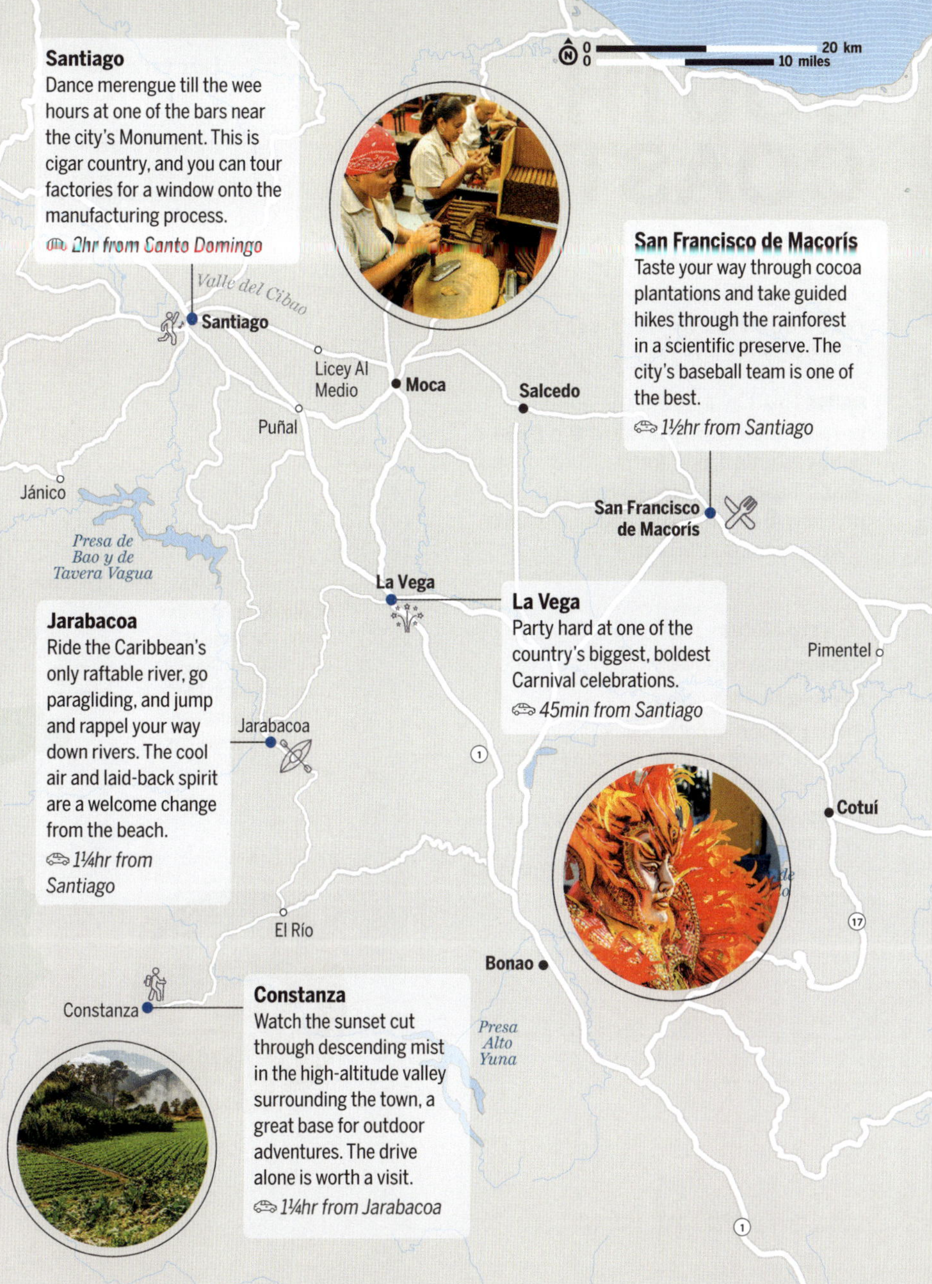
0 20 km
0 10 miles
Santiago
Dance merengue till the wee hours at one of the bars near the city's Monument. This is cigar country, and you can tour factories for a window onto the manufacturing process.
2hr from Santo Domingo
San Francisco de Macorís
Taste your way through cocoa plantations and take guided hikes through the rainforest in a scientific preserve. The city's baseball team is one of the best.
1½hr from Santiago
Valle del Cibao
Santiago
Licey Al Medio
Moca
Salcedo
Puñal
Jánico
San Francisco de Macorís
Presa de Bao y de Tavera Vagua
La Vega
La Vega
Party hard at one of the country's biggest, boldest Carnival celebrations.
45min from Santiago
Jarabacoa
Ride the Caribbean's only raftable river, go paragliding, and jump and rappel your way down rivers. The cool air and laid-back spirit are a welcome change from the beach.
1¼hr from Santiago
Pimentel
Jarabacoa
1
Cotuí
17
El Río
Bonao
Constanza
Constanza
Watch the sunset cut through descending mist in the high-altitude valley surrounding the town, a great base for outdoor adventures. The drive alone is worth a visit.
1¼hr from Jarabacoa
Presa Alto Yuna
1

SOUTH COAST
Trip Builder

TAKE YOUR PICK OF MUST-SEES AND HIDDEN GEMS

Head away from the populous parts of the country, toward the DR's wilder western side for far-flung offshore island beaches, remote parks and preserves, and massive lagoons where wildlife reigns supreme.

Trip Notes

Hub towns San Cristóbal

How long Allow five days

Getting around Rent your vehicle in Santo Domingo. Strongly consider getting a 4WD for less-than-stellar roads.

Tips March and April are the best times to see birds and wildlife. On the coast south of Barahona, hotels perch on dramatic coastline; Pedernales has gorgeous glamping.

Lago Enriquillo
Admire beefy iguanas, crocodiles, turtles and dozens of bird species (including flamingos) at an inland saltwater lake.
1½hr from Barahona

109
1
Port-au-Prince
Pétionville
Kenscoff
HAITI
Jacmel
Pedernales

Bahía de las Águilas
Drink in paradise at the DR's most blissful and deserted beach. The boat ride out past cliffs with diving pelicans is worth the journey.
1¼hr from Laguna Oviedo

FROM TOP: NEIL BOWMAN/SHUTTERSTOCK, ZUMA PRESS, INC/ALAMY, JOEL LEGER/SHUTTERSTOCK, ONAPALMTREE/SHUTTERSTOCK

Parque Nacional Sierra de Bahoruco

Take a gander at a stunning gorge overlook and pull out your binoculars for birding in a mountainous cloud forest.

1hr from Barahona

San Cristóbal

Explore one of the best places to see millennia-old rock art and an off-beat museum dedicated to a dark period of Dominican history.

30min from Santo Domingo

Laguna Oviedo

Spot flamingos and turtles on a boat tour of this super-salty lagoon. Colonies of other bird species make this one of the country's top spots for bird-watching.

1¾hr from Barahona

Islas Beata & Alto Velo

Brave the waves out to these offshore islands, rich in sea and shore birds, and protected by the Parque Nacional Jaragua.

2hr from Playa Las Cuevas

7 Things to Know About the DOMINICAN REPUBLIC

INSIDER TIPS TO HIT THE GROUND RUNNING

1 Drinking Etiquette

When toasting shots in a group, it's customary to say: *'¡Pa' rriba!'* (Up!), *'¡Pa' abajo!'* (Down!), *'¡Pa'l centro!'* (To the center!), *'¡Pa' dentro!'* (Get it in!) and *'Salud'* for cheers. There's a saying that goes, 'Brugal gets the party started, but Macorix keeps it going,' in reference to two Dominican brands of rum; the latter is generally considered to be of better quality.

2 Car Service Apps

Taxis can be pricey. In places like Punta Cana, fares are basically fixed. Elsewhere, negotiate hard. Uber is widely used, most extensively in big cities. InDrive is an alternative app: cash-only, it involves riders placing 'bids' on routes that can be accepted (or not) from drivers. All-inclusive resorts don't allow car service hires to access their properties.

3 Budgeting

Bring all the sunscreen, bug repellent, and so on that you'll need. Of course, these can be found at shops everywhere, but are likely be much pricier than at home, especially at all-inclusive resort shops.

4 Phones & Messaging

Everything runs on WhatsApp. If you don't already have it, install it prior to arrival. Wi-fi can be spotty; even in resorts, no matter the level of luxury. Keep this in mind if you depend on it for work purposes.

5 Tipping

Carry plenty of US$1 (and, to a lesser extent, US$5) bills to tip for services, guides or taxi drivers; especially useful if staying at all-inclusive resorts. Every bill at a restaurant, cafe or bar will be increased by a whopping 28%! This includes an 18% sales tax and 10% service charge. There's no obligation to add anything more; however, some people leave another 10% in Dominican pesos for service above and beyond.

▶ See p237 for more about money

6 All-Inclusive Insights

All-inclusives are, on the whole, extremely good value. The highest-priced properties aren't necessarily the nicest, but the food quality at lower-cost options is generally mediocre at best. Book reservations for 'special' restaurants immediately upon arrival. At these, take waitstaff dish recommendations with a grain of salt: they might be pushing the lowest-cost options.

Bring at least one 'formal' outfit for higher-end dining; many have dress codes that are enforced. Your own large tumbler can come in handy for drinks at resort beach and pool bars, where otherwise they're served in small plastic cups.

Pay attention to detailed location information, especially if it's not described as 'beachfront.' The quality of beaches can vary dramatically; check out photos before booking.

You have to check out in person. Procedures and lines can be long, so allow enough time if a flight is involved.

▶ See p100 for more all-inclusive information

7 Airport Tips

Visitors must fill out a free online registration form prior to arrival in and departure from the DR (eticket.migracion.gob.do). Complete both before arriving and, if possible, print out copies. Don't click on alternative links: these could be scams asking for payment. When boarding flights in the DR, ask at check-in for a printed boarding pass. Sometimes, security doesn't accept digital versions.

▶ See p232 for more arrival information

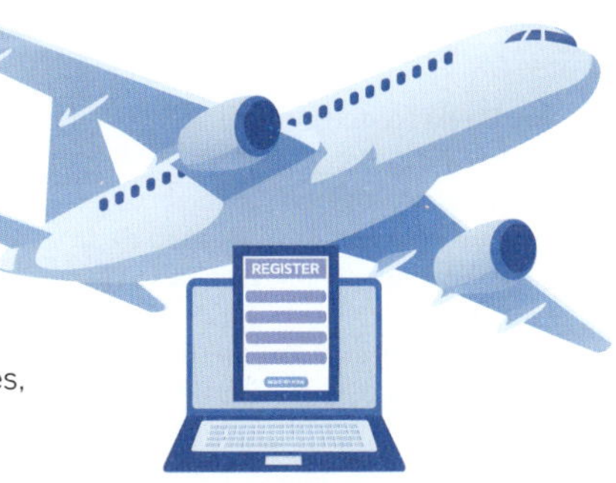

Read, Listen, Watch & Follow

READ

Dead Man in Paradise (JB MacKinnon; 2005) Canadian journalist pieces together an unsolved murder under Trujillo.

East of Haiti: Three Novellas (César Sánchez Beras; 2024) Stories of characters struggles with their identities.

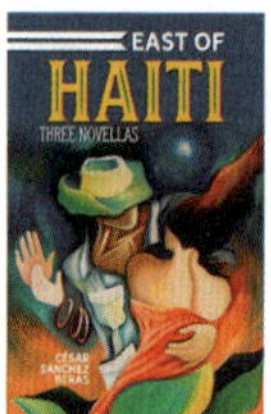

The Dictator Next Door (Eric Paul Roorda; 1998) Explores the US government's complicity with Trujillo's regime.

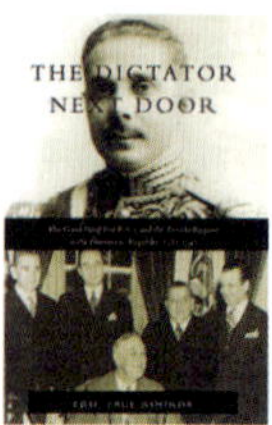

Feast of the Goat (Mario Vargas Llosa; 2000) Exceptional imagining of dictator Trujillo's final days.

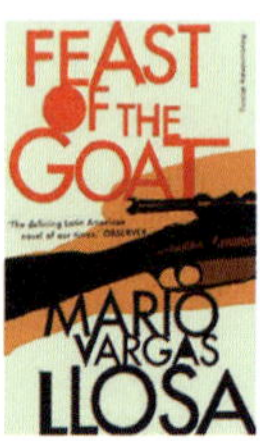

LISTEN

RD: República Decadente (La Ñapa; 2016) Experimental audio project satirizing politics and life in the DR.

Voy Pa'lla (Antony Santos, pictured; 1991) Debut single considered one of the most influential *bachata* songs; helped establish Santos' fame.

Bachata Roja (various artists; 1990) Classic bachata from the early 1960s to late 1980s, the pre-electric era when the music was entirely guitar based.

Rumbo de la mañana Weekly podcast focused on culture and current events; in Spanish.

DAN HERRICK/ZUMA WIRE/ALAMY

Mi Derriengue (Riccie Oriach; 2020) Incredibly eclectic album mixing nearly every Dominican music style, as well as punk, rock and funk.

WATCH

Liborio (2021) Art-house tale based on the life of a historical Dominican faith healer during 1910 US occupation.

Perico Ripiao (2003) Comedy about three musically talented escaped criminals and their high jinks on journey home.

Machete Gillette... Mama (1998) Avant-garde impressionistic documentary about filmmaker Larry Gottheim's travels in the DR.

Hotel Coppelia (2021) Set in a brothel during the 1965 US invasion of the DR amid social and political collapse. Directed by José María Cabral (pictured center, right).

Cocote (2017) Original and stylistic tale of a son who faces pressure to avenge his father's death.

SIPA USA/ALAMY

FOLLOW

godominican republic.com
DR Tourism's official site with news, trends and stories.

Everyday Dominican
(@everyday.dr)
Visual window onto Dominicans' daily lives.

Dominican Cooking
(dominicancooking.com) Culture and cooking with recipes galore.

Jamie Gruber
(@thejamiegruber)
Helpful, opinionated videos covering travel, daily life, etc.

American in the DR
(meemselle.wordpress.com) An expat's life in the DR.

Sate your Dominican Republic dreaming with a virtual vacation

SANTO
DOMINGO
HISTORY | CULTURE | FOOD
Experience
Santo
Domingo
online

SANTO DOMINGO
Trip Builder

A collage of neighborhoods, 'La Capital' is an intensely urban city with a typically Dominican laid-back spirit. Santo Domingo's streets are alive, home to hot clubs, bustling cafes and markets – a living museum crossed with a seaside resort with the historically dense Zona Colonial at its heart.

Root for the home team at the country's premier **baseball stadium** (p58)
25min from Zona Colonial

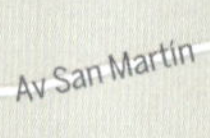

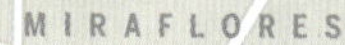

Brush up on Dominican art, history and culture at **Plaza de la Cultura** (p73)
10min from Zona Colonial

Dance away a Sunday night to classic merengue, *bachata* and *son* (Cuban-style) tunes at **Grupo Bonyé** (p63)
10min from Catedral Primada de América

Shop the Zona Colonia's **Mercado Modelo** and boutiques for the perfect souvenir (p66)
15min from Catedral Primada de América

Browse the shelves of **Librería Mamey**, a charming bookstore and cultural center (p67)
10min from Catedral Primada de América

Step back through the centuries along **Calle las Damas**, the oldest-surviving paved street in the Americas (p52)
2min from Parque Colón

Learn about one of the darkest periods in the country's history at **Museo Memorial de la Resistencia Dominicana** (p57)
5min from Catedral Primada de América

Admire the architectural evolution of **Catedral Primada de América**, the oldest cathedral in the Americas (p51)
2min from Fortaleza Ozama

FROM LEFT: NURPHOTO/GETTY IMAGES, HACKENBERG-PHOTO-COLOGNE/ALAMY, HACKENBERG-PHOTO-COLOGNE/ALAMY, FLORIN CNEJEVICI/SHUTTERSTOCK. PREVIOUS SPREAD: ERIKA SANTELICES/GETTY IMAGES

Practicalities

LEONARD ZHUKOVSKY/SHUTTERSTOCK

ARRIVING

Aeropuerto Internacional De Las Américas The city's major airport for international flights is 26km east of Zona Colonial. A taxi into the city costs US$40 to US$50; an Uber is around US$20. You can walk around 100m to the right of baggage claim and grab a *motoconcho* (motorcycle taxi) to take you to a *guagua* (local bus) stop on the highway.

HOW MUCH FOR A

Cocktail
RD$260

Sancocho (stew)
RD$480

Espadrilles
US$50

GETTING AROUND

Driving Driving isn't for the faint of heart in Santo Domingo; it's a free-for-all with little attention to road rules. The most convenient and safest way to maneuver is to use Uber or Cabify, another rideshare app.

Público Old buses and typically beaten-up minivans stop whenever flagged down: hold out your arm and point down at the curb in front of you.

Metro The metro system is modern and clean. Line 1 runs north to south; Line 2 runs east to west. The 5km Teleférico Santo Domingo cable car line connects 23 districts on both sides of the Río Ozama.

WHEN TO GO

JAN–MAR
Carnival, at the end of February and beginning of March, is a big deal.

APR–JUN
In between seasons means lower accommodations costs.

JUL–SEP
Hurricane season means strong rains are a threat, but sunshine is common.

OCT–DEC
Baseball at Estadio Quisqueya from the end of October through January.

EATING & DRINKING

Santo Domingo is the culinary and nightlife capital of the country. This is where ambitious homegrown chefs come to make their bones with innovatively imagined tapas infused with Dominican flavors, while streetside vendors hawk no-less-delicious empanadas and chicharron (salty, crunchy pork rind; pictured top right). From *pastelitos* (pastries with meat, vegetable or seafood fillings; picture bottom right) to extravagantly prepared seafood meals, Dominican cuisine is on the menu.

Best late-night snack
Barra Payán (p75)

Must-try rum
Sugarcane, La Casa del Ron (p74)

TOP: EZUME IMAGES/SHUTTERSTOCK
BOTTOM: MARIO DE MOYA F/SHUTTERSTOCK

CONNECT & FIND YOUR WAY

Wi-fi Hotels, cafes and restaurants have good reception. Buy a SIM card from Claro or Altice (data-only; at the airport or electronics stores).

Navigation The Zona Colonial is wonderfully easy and pleasurable to navigate on foot. The city's southern boundary fronts the Caribbean along the Malecón and the Río Ozama divides the city into east and west.

SAFETY

Be extra cautious if you've been drinking or you're leaving a club at night, to avoid becoming a robbery target. Ubers are the safest means of transportation.

WHERE TO STAY

Most travelers choose to stay in the Zona Colonial, the city's most distinctive neighborhood with a wide range of accommodations, many in beautifully restored colonial-era buildings.

Place	Pros/Cons
Zona Colonial	Close to important historic sites; walkable; loads of restaurants, cafes and bars. Pools are rare.
Malecón	Sea views; resort-style high-rises with pools. You'll need taxis and Ubers to get elsewhere.
Downtown	Several shopping malls and chic chain hotels; good restaurants within short drives. Heavy traffic and noise; not a distinctive neighborhood.
Gazcue	Quiet residential neighborhood with limited options.

MONEY

You can find *casas de cambio* (money changers) on Calle El Conde. Paying in cash pesos is the most economical way to go. There are several major banks with ATMs in the Zona Colonial.

01 A WANDER Through History

ARCHITECTURE | STREET LIFE

Founded in 1496, Santo Domingo is the oldest continuously inhabited European settlement in the Americas. Traces of its early years remain in the 11 lively, history-filled blocks of the UNESCO World Heritage–listed Zona Colonial, situated on the west bank of the Río Ozama.

MAREMAGNUM/GETTY IMAGES

How To

Getting around This mostly flat, compact area is laid out on a grid and is entirely and enjoyably walkable.

When to go The most pleasant temperatures might be November to March, but the city's Carnival in late February is the country's biggest blowout.

Old-world lodgings Some of the city's nicest boutique accommodations can be found in the Zona Colonial's restored historic buildings dating from the 16th to 18th centuries.

Oldest Cathedral in the Americas

Time stands still for no one, especially not for prime real estate – not even for the oldest surviving cathedral in the Americas. The incongruity of the **Catedral Primada de América**'s location at the heart of the neighborhood – surrounded by buoyant cafes, rooftop rum bars and a Hard Rock Cafe, and fronted by a pigeon-clogged public plaza – only heightens the improbability of its survival. With the first stone set in 1514 by Diego Columbus, son of Christopher (the ashes of both once supposedly rested in the chapel's crypt), and used by English privateer Sir Francis Drake and his crew as headquarters during their 1586 assault on the city, you'll truly wish 'these walls could talk.' A number of architects worked on the building over time, which is why the vault

PACK-SHOT/SHUTTERSTOCK

Left Interior of Catedral Primada de América **Top left** Fortaleza Ozama (p53)

is Gothic, the arches are Romanesque and the ornamentation is baroque. Purchase the audio guide (available in a variety of languages) to learn more about its story.

Other Record Breakers

Running north–south in front of Fortaleza Ozama, **Calle las Damas** is the oldest surviving colonial paved street in the Americas. Laid in 1502, the street acquired its name from the wife of Diego Columbus and her lady friends, who strolled the road every afternoon.

Standing next to the bright, white Iglesia de la Altagracia are the ruins of the **Hospital San Nicolás de Barí**, the first colonial hospital in the Americas. They remain as a monument to Governor Nicolás de Ovando, who ordered the hospital built in 1503. Devastated by a hurricane in 1911, much of it was knocked down so that it wouldn't pose a threat to pedestrians.

Pirate of the Caribbean

During its early years, Santo Domingo's fortunes rose and fell on the whims of kings and queens an ocean away. In 1586, with tensions between the Spanish and English monarchs running high, English privateer Sir Francis Drake launched a preemptive strike against the Spanish colony, capturing the city and holding it hostage. Besides ransacking the cathedral, Drake and his men sacked the Iglesia de Santa Clara and set the Monasterio de San Francisco ablaze. The Casa del Cordón is believed to be the site where Santo Domingo's women lined up to hand over their jewels to Drake. The month-long siege ended when Drake collected a ransom and returned the city to Spanish control.

Oldest Colonial Fort

What appears to be an anomalous medieval-style castle guarding the industrialized port of the western bank of the Río Ozama is in fact **Fortaleza Ozama**, the oldest colonial military edifice in the Americas. Some of the buildings, built largely by African slaves and indigenous forced labor, date to the early 1500s.

MEHDI KASUMOV/SHUTTERSTOCK

Said to be not only one of the first European residences in the Americas, but also one of the first to have two floors, the **Casa del Cordón** was briefly occupied by Diego Columbus and his wife before they moved into their stately home down the street. Today, the structure is home to Banco Popular, so visiting beyond the main lobby isn't permitted.

Built in 1510 by Charles V, the **Convento de los Dominicos** is the first convent of the Dominican order founded in the Americas. It's also where Father Bartolomé de las Casas – the chronicler of Spanish atrocities against indigenous peoples – did most of his writing.

Not to be outdone, the **Iglesia de Santa Clara** is home to the first nunnery in the Americas, built in 1552. The imposing whitewashed facade has a severe Renaissance-style portal with a gable containing a bust of St Claire.

The **Monasterio de San Francisco**, the first monastery in the Americas, belonged to the first order of Franciscan friars who arrived to evangelize the island. Originally dating from 1508, it was rebuilt several times over the centuries after being devastated by a number of earthquakes; today, its ruins are the scene of wild dance nights every Sunday (see p63).

FROM LEFT: ORIOLE GIN/SHUTTERSTOCK, ADRIAN GRIFFITH/ALAMY

Left Hospital San Nicolás de Barí
Top Fortaleza Ozama
Above Monasterio de San Francisco

HISTORICAL/GETTY IMAGES

The Rise of the Caudillo

PAR FOR THE COURSE: POLITICAL INSTABILITY AND INFLUENCE

Ever since Columbus landed on Hispaniola in 1492, the DR has seen wave after wave of foreign interlopers. But in the early 20th century, the country was indelibly marked by a homegrown dictator and US influence.

Left Portrait of Buenaventura Báez
Center Portrait of Ulises Heureaux
Right Rafael L Trujillo

Imperial Power to the North

Soon after the Dominican Republic gained its independence from Spain for the second time in 1865 (the first was in 1821), its newly formed, barely functioning government faced the first of 50 military coups that would take place over the next 14 years, resulting in 21 changes of government. One of these coalitions, led by Buenaventura Báez, who was installed as president, sought to sell the country to the US for roughly US$150,000 in 1869. Remarkably, the agreement, later rejected by the US Senate, was signed by Báez and US President Ulysses S Grant.

From 1882, some stability returned, if at the hands of military leader General Ulises Heureaux, who was assassinated in 1899. But in order to finance the army, infrastructure and sugar industry, Heureaux borrowed from American and European banks. Following a massive drop in world sugar prices, Heureaux essentially mortgaged the DR to a US-owned and operated company. In 1905, the US government, under President Theodore Roosevelt, intervened, taking over Dominican customs and guaranteeing repayment of loans. Instability, corruption and the assassination of another Dominican president followed, until 1916, when US President Woodrow Wilson sent in the US marines, ostensibly to stop another coup. They controversially remained, along with 3000 other troops, for eight years – long after the country's chaotic political situation and economy had improved.

The occupation ended only with the emergence of a new spirit of American isolationism and a lessening of the DR's strategic value.

OLD BOOKS IMAGES/ALAMY

BETTMANN/GETTY IMAGES

Trujillo, the Dictator

Six years of relatively stable government followed, led by progressive president Horacio Vásquez. Roads and schools were built and irrigation and sanitation programs initiated. However, in a constitutionally questionable move approved by the Congress, Vásquez extended his four-year term to six years.

Trujillo ruled the Dominican Republic for the next 30 years, suppressing and punishing dissent through massive investment in and expansion of the Guardia Nacional and intelligence agencies.

Revolutionary sentiments, never far from the surface, erupted again in 1930. Rafael Leónidas Trujillo, chief of the former Dominican National Police (renamed the National Army in 1928), ordered his troops to remain in their barracks, effectively forcing the administration to fold. A sham election followed, with Trujillo the sole candidate.

Within weeks, Trujillo organized a terrorist band called La 42 that roamed the country killing everyone who posed any threat to him. A narcissist of the first degree, he changed the names of various cities – Santo Domingo became Ciudad Trujillo – and lavished support on San Cristóbal, the small city in the west where he was born. Trujillo ruled the Dominican Republic for the next 30 years, suppressing and punishing dissent through massive investment in and expansion of the Guardia Nacional and intelligence agencies.

Political prisoners and opposition figures were tortured and murdered. The most infamous atrocity was the 1937 Parsley

An Authoritarian by Any Name

Life in Santo Domingo during the Trujillo regime was regimented: begging was only allowed on Saturdays, laborers were awakened with a 7am siren, while office workers, given an extra hour of sleep, had a 8am siren. Trujillo had several nicknames, including Hot Balls, the Goat, the Chief, the Butcher, as well as holding multiple titles: Benefactor of the Fatherland, Founder and Supreme Chief of the Partido Dominicana, Restorer of Financial Independence, First Journalist of the Republic and Doctor Honoris Causa in the Economic Political Sciences, to name just a few.

Massacre of tens of thousands of Haitians along the DR–Haiti border. Trujillo, despite having African ancestry, was deeply racist and xenophobic and sought to 'whiten' the DR by increasing European immigration and placing strict quotas on Haitian immigration.

Trujillo used his power to amass a personal fortune, establishing monopolies controlled by his family. By 1934 he was the richest man on the island. Some Dominicans still refer to Trujillo's rule with fondness and nostalgia, in part because factories were opened, a number of grand infrastructure and public works projects were carried out, and bridges and highways were built.

Trujillo used his power to amass a personal fortune, establishing monopolies controlled by his family.

Never-ending Unrest

When Trujillo was assassinated by a group of Dominican dissidents with the support of the CIA on May 30, 1961, some hoped the country would turn a corner. The promise of change, however, was short-lived. After Trujillo's son, Ramfis, assumed the presidency, a power struggle with Joaquín Balaguer erupted. Ramfis fled the country and Balaguer gained the title of president (he would serve three non-consecutive terms). Balaguer wasn't the typical authoritarian dictator in one respect: he was a poet and writer. However, there's little subtext or guessing his beliefs – in one book he argues against interracial marriage.

After a groundswell of unrest and at the insistence of the USA, a seven-member Council of State was established to guide the country until elections were held in December 1962. The first free election in many years was won by the scholar-poet Juan Bosch Gaviño.

Nine months later, in September 1963, after introducing liberal policies including the redistribution of land, the creation of a new constitution and guaranteeing civil and individual rights, Bosch was deposed by yet another military coup. Wealthy landowners, to whom democracy was a threat, and a group of military leaders led by Generals Elías Wessin y Wessin and Antonio Imbert Barreras installed Donald Reid Cabral, a prominent businessman, as president. Bosch fled into exile but his supporters, calling themselves the Constitutionalists, took to the streets and seized the National Palace. Santo Domingo saw the stirrings of a civil war as the military launched tank assaults and bombing runs against civilian protesters.

WORLD HISTORY ARCHIVE/ALAMY

KEYSTONE PRESS/ALAMY

MUSEO MEMORIAL DE LA ESISTENCIA DOMINICANA

SOMAN · OWN WORK/WIKIMEDIA/CC BY-SA 3.0

Occupation Redux

The fighting continued until the USA intervened again. The Lyndon B Johnson administration feared a left-wing or communist takeover of the Dominican Republic, largely without reason: Bosch wasn't a communist and it was later revealed US intelligence had identified only a few dozen individuals fighting the military junta. The official reason was that the US could no longer guarantee the safety of its nationals and so over 500 marines landed in Santo Domingo on April 27, 1965. A week later, and only 40 years since the previous occupation, 14,000 American military personnel were stationed in the Dominican Republic. Eventually, over 42,000 US troops were involved in an occupation that ended 14 months later, with a new, more conservative government installed and elections in the offing.

Deepen Your Understanding

For those interested in learning more about the details of one of country's darkest periods, head to the **Museo Memorial de la Resistencia Dominicana** in Zona Colonial. Understandably austere, the museum honors Dominicans who fought against 'El Chivo' (The Goat) Rafael Trujillo, the brutal dictator who ruled with an iron fist from 1930 until 1961, touting his own greatness and wiping out some 50,000 political dissenters. The museum features torture-center replicas and 160,000 photographs, films and other objects belonging to resistance fighters. Admission includes an audio guide (English or Spanish).

Far left Car in which Rafael Trujillo was assassinated **Left** Armed Dominican troops disperse rioters, 1963 **Top left** Display at Museo Memorial de la Resistencia Dominicana **Top right** Exterior of Museo Memorial de la Resistencia Dominicana

02 Take Me Out to the BALL GAME

SPECTATOR SPORTS | CULTURE | DRINKS

Rivaling Catholicism, the family and merengue as the cultural glue that holds all Dominicans together, is baseball. While most players aspire to the bright lights and big bucks of the US major leagues, the DR's homegrown teams have an entire nation as their passionate fan base, and games here feature better dancers and a wider selection of stadium fare.

WIRESTOCK CREATORS/SHUTTERSTOCK

How To

When to go The season begins at the end of October, culminating in a championship series at the end of January.

Where Estadio Quisqueya (Av Tiradentes 3456) is home to two (longtime rivals) of the country's five teams. Games are played several nights a week.

Getting tickets Arrive early to buy tickets at the box office or try online at uepatickets.com/tickets/principal. Showing up to the stadium not long before first pitch means buying from scalpers; be wary, as costs quoted are usually three to four times face value.

FELIX LEON/GETTY IMAGES

FEDERICO PARRA/GETTY IMAGES

Far left bottom Leones del Escogido's team manager Albert Pujols **Far left top** Estadio Quisqueya Juan Marichal **Left** Tigres del Licey fans

Field of Sueños Santo Domingo's **Estadio Quisqueya Juan Marichal** (known simply as Estadio Quisqueya) is the DR's biggest stage, where young stars are born and veterans return, often from the USA's Major League Baseball, for a final go in the pros. You might be surprised by some of the names you recognize – Albert Pujols and Yasiel Puig are notable examples in recent years. Homefield to both Tigres del Licey and Leones del Escojido, games between these two teams sell out more quickly than others. Asking at the box office for best seats available should put you close to the action.

Join the Party Fans get decked out in their team colors, waving pennants and flags, as rabidly partisan as the Yankees vs Red Sox. Things can get festively loud and raucous, possibly due to the *chinola*-based alcoholic drinks (essentially a passion fruit liqueur), cheap bottles of Presidente beer and bottles of rum for sale. Fresh mango, fried plantains and corn on the cob are sold outside, with empanadas and more sold by roving vendors inside. Cheerleaders dance on top of the clubhouse in between innings, often in a style some might describe as less-than-family-friendly. The stadium's long center field (125m/411ft) means home runs have to be tagged to leave the yard.

The Other Beautiful Game

Still a dim flicker on the national consciousness, there's a growing interest in Latin America's and the rest of the world's most popular sport: soccer. The Liga Dominicana de Futbol, the DR's pro league, comprises 12 teams and plays from late August to May. In recent years the sport's profile has increased: in 2023, construction began on a large new stadium at Cap Cana, in the nation's southeast, and in 2024, the national men's team competed in the Paris Olympics, though they didn't make it out of the group stage.

Play Ball, in the DR

BASEBALL, THE COUNTRY'S OTHER RELIGION

Not just the USA's game, *béisbol* is an integral part of the Dominican social and cultural landscape. So much so that Dominican ballplayers who have made good in the US, like David Ortiz and Sammy Sosa, are without doubt the most popular and revered figures in the country.

Left High-school kids play baseball **Center** Players in the Boston Red Sox Dominican Republic Baseball Academy warm up **Right** David Ortiz

ROBERT NICKELSBERG/GETTY IMAGES

Baseball's Beginnings

At first glance a seemingly unrelated pairing, sugar and baseball both got their starts in the DR at around the same time and their origins are inextricably linked. Just as US business ambitions were directed toward the Caribbean (and Cuba, in particular), baseball was being established in the United States. When Cuban plantation owners fled Cuba for the DR during the failed 1868 war of independence, they brought their passion for the game, which they learned from the Americans. English-speaking Caribbean people who were brought to the DR to work in the cane fields were already skilled at cricket and the associated general concepts of batting, pitching and fielding. With few leisure activities available, plant owners encouraged baseball and organized teams into a competitive 'sugar league.' Cubans, Americans and Dominicans in Santo Domingo, La Vega and near Santiago also formed teams. The US embargo of Cuba that began in 1962 (as well as free agency, which began in the 1970s) jump-started the recruitment of Dominican players into the US Major League.

Pitfall-Filled Road to Riches

The financial incentives for a young prospect in the DR of just being drafted, let alone actually playing in the Major League, are substantial. Signing bonuses can reach many millions of US dollars: life-changing amounts and more than enough to help support extended family. However, the odds are overwhelmingly against success – only 3% of those signed make it to the majors – and when a young

BOSTON GLOBE/GETTY IMAGES

UPI/ALAMY

teenager pins their hopes on baseball (players are eligible for recruitment, often with verbal agreements and money exchanging hands before the age of 16), education usually falls by the wayside. A series of high-profile issues have arisen, complicating the close relationship between Dominican baseball and the Major League (Dominicans make up 10% of opening day rosters).

> Signing bonuses can reach many millions of US dollars: life-changing amounts and more than enough to help support extended family.

Nearly every team has an academy here – a mix of university dormitory, work camp and health club. Problems include steroid use, which isn't technically illegal in the DR (and can be bought at pharmacies without prescriptions), fake birth certificates intentionally misstating a player's age (younger to overstate potential and older to allow recruitment) and the increasingly questionable role that unregulated *buscones* play in the whole system. Taken from the Spanish verb *'buscar'* (to look for), *buscones* are more than merely scouts. They train, feed, house and educate promising players, grooming them to be signed by the MLB in the hopes of one day gaining a large percentage of whatever signing bonus their prospects earn. According to critics, the legacy of this corruption helps explain why around 50% of players (major and minor leaguers) caught violating the drug policy, mostly with anabolic steroids, since 2005 are Dominicans.

Hall of Dominican Legends

Major League Baseball's Hall of Fame is located in bucolic Cooperstown, New York. Plans for the Dominican Republic's own Hall of Fame, still in the funding stage, are for a location in sunnier, warmer climes along the Autopista del Coral in Punta Cana. The sports synergy between the two countries means the museum and the already functioning foundation emphasize the legacy of Dominican players who have made good in the US (Osvaldo Virgil, Felipe Alou, Juan Marichal, Sammy Sosa, David Ortiz and Albert Pujols to name only a few) as much as in the DR's own highly talented pro league.

03 Nightlife CAPITAL

MUSIC | DRINKS | NEIGHBORHOODS

Santo Domingo absolutely knows how to throw down – just look at the *colmados,* corner stores where people imbibe and socialize all day and all night. But *la capital* is where the highest-profile musicians play, from glitzy nightclubs to intimate spaces drawing a cross-section of Dominicans.

VW PICS/GETTY IMAGES

How To

Did you know? Car washes in the DR satisfy two passions – cars and beer. Drinks are served throughout the afternoon and evening.

Getting there Zona Colonial bars can be navigated on foot, but it's best to be in a group late at night. Catch an Uber to and from all other destinations.

What to order Associated with the Cocolo community around San Pedro de Macorís, guavaberry cocktail is one of DR's signature drinks: a combo of sugarcane, rum and guavaberries.

LARRY MARANO/SHUTTERSTOCK

Party Like a Local

One of the city's most undeniably, maybe even universally, appealing, nightlife scenes is the Sunday night **Grupo Bonyé** party held outdoors in front of the ruins of the Zona Colonial's Monasterio de San Francisco from 6pm to 10pm. The welcoming, joyful vibe will have even the most dance averse moving to the classic merengue, *bachata* and *son* tunes blasted from speakers. It's free, unless you arrive early to 'reserve' one of the plastic tables for a small fee. Bring your own beer or grab one from a roving vendor; cheap empanadas and other snacks are also sold. Grab one of the plastic chairs perched on the rim of the monastery's crumbling walls for balcony-like views of the dancing in the courtyard below.

It's a singularly Dominican scene, loose and proud, and even more unique when you

MATYAS REHAK/SHUTTERSTOCK

Big Names in Merengue

Some of the most popular merengue musicians include Johnny Ventura, Cocoband, Wilfrido Vargas, Milly y los Vecinos, Fernando Villalona, Joseíto Mateo, Rubby Pérez, Miriam Cruz, Milly Quezada and, perhaps the biggest name of all, Santo Domingo–born Juan Luis Guerra.

Left Local *colmado* **Top left** Grupo Bonyé party **Above** Juan Luis Guerra

consider the setting: the first monastery established in the Americas, dating to 1508. Another interesting historical note: this surely wouldn't have been allowed in 1818 when the Spanish colonial governor ordered nighttime dancing in the street without a permit to be illegal.

Nights in La Zona

Restaurants and cafes along Plaza España, the eastern end of Calle El Conde, and Plazoleta Padre Billini are all happening spots after dark.

Hasta la Tambora, run by Dominican music legend Henry Jiménez, not only serves some of the best drinks in the neighborhood (all named after well-known merengue songs), but it also has live music nightly. It's an infectious scene that shouldn't be missed.

Oasis Bar & Lounge, perched on a cliff in the Zona Colonial, is more of a local's spot.

Music Genres

Life in Santo Domingo, like elsewhere in the DR, moves to a background soundtrack of infectious rhythms, but it's not all merengue, *bachata* and salsa. Reggaeton, a mix of American-style hip-hop and Latin rhythms with a distinctly urban flavor, exploded onto the Dominican scene several decades ago. Its fast-paced danceable beats, street-life narratives and catchy choruses make it the party music of choice for young Dominicans.

Dembow, another genre with a similar origin story, has grown in popularity over the last two decades. Its sped-up rhythms and beats, musically more simple, derive their power through repetition and lyrics, heavy on slang, and focused on *barrio* (neighborhood) life.

Left Street cafes in La Zona
Below Santo Domingo at night

Other Avenidas

Drinking holes are everywhere, but there are several areas to home in on. Many of the nicer bars are in strip malls around the city in Piantini and Naco. No T-shirts, sneakers or sandals; dress in your finest.

The Malecón, which runs for 14km along the city's waterfront, is dotted with nightclubs, several of which are in high-rise hotels. In April 2025, tragedy struck when the roof of Jet Set, one of the area's longest-running and highest-profile merengue clubs, collapsed. Over 100 people were killed, including merengue great Rubby Pérez.

Along Av Rómulo Betancourt, east out near Parque Mirador del Sur, places like **La Otra Bar & Lounge**, **Brickell Rooftop** and **Piso 84 Rooftop Bar** combine views, good food, drinks and live music. Along Av Gustavo Mejia Ricart, you'll find **La Posta Bar**, **Maruja Bar** and plenty of others.

Clubs in Santo Domingo Este, on the eastern side of the Río Ozama, see few tourists; however, there are plenty of clubs clustered around Av Venezuela.

04 SHOP 'Til You Drop

CRAFTS | MARKETS | LOCAL LIFE

Forget the cheap tourist kitsch that touts push to crowds fresh off cruise ships and the upscale massive malls downtown (worth visiting for necessities) – Santo Domingo is an under-the-radar destination for quality collectibles and ateliers of independent-minded designers.

How To

Getting there You'll need to take a taxi or Uber to get to shops and markets outside the Zona Colonial.

Best buy Mamajuana, a drink made from rum, red wine, and honey soaked in tree bark and herbs. Or pick up a premade blend of special ingredients from a souvenir shop (RD$400 to RD$600) and make your own: add rum, some wine, mix, let sit and enjoy.

Opening hours Most shops are closed on Sundays; however, malls and supermarkets stay open.

Casual Browsing in Zona Colonial

One long commercial walkway, **Calle el Conde** runs east–west through the heart of Zona Colonial. It's a necessary stroll to get the pulse of the neighborhood; however, the shops are primarily for everyday goods, clothing and the hawking of cheap, mass-produced 'Haitian'-style paintings, jewelry and the like. One-stop **Mercado Modelo** (9am-6pm, to 1pm Sun) has plenty of stalls that cater to tourists with mass-produced 'Caribbean' handicrafts and paintings, but you can also find cigars,

Top right Handmade espadrilles on display at La Alpargatería

LA ALPARGATERÍA

liquor (including mamajuana), and other gifts to take back home. Bargain, because you'll be initially quoted an excessive price.

Just north of the Zona Colonial, along Av Duarte, is the city's **Chinatown**; on Sundays, fresh produce is sold from street stalls. Massive malls can be found throughout the city.

Dominican Stones

If you are considering buying something in amber or Larimar (the DR's unique pale-blue stone), shop around since these stones, considered national treasures, are virtually ubiquitous in Santo Domingo. Typically, they're presented as jewelry, but occasionally you'll find figurines, rosaries and other small objects. Quality and price vary greatly and fakes aren't uncommon. In Zona Colonial, the most recommended places are the **Amber World Museum** and the **Larimar Museum**.

Ateliers, Designers & Culture Favorites

Casa Alfarera Beyond being a beautiful ceramics studio, it really reflects the essence of local craftsmanship. Everything feels authentic and thoughtfully made.

Quinta Dominica A peaceful cultural oasis with a cafe, exhibitions and a shop that feels more curated than commercial.

La Alpargatería Artisan handmade espadrilles in the heart of the Zona Colonial.

Librería Mamey A charming independent bookstore and small cultural center; it's a perfect place to slow down, browse and get a sense of the city's creative pulse.

Indómita A lively space that promotes up-and-coming Dominican designers, offering everything from fashion to home decor with a fresh perspective.

Recommended by Ricardo Fernández, *co-owner of La Alpargatería @laalpargateria*

DON'T LEAVE
Santo Domingo Without

01 Coffee
Grown in six different regions by over 60,000 growers, coffee is a staple of any menu and most Dominicans' diets.

02 Dominoes set
With only slightly different rules to the international game, Dominican dominoes are played everywhere, often on streetside tables.

03 Bottle of mamajuana
DR's own homemade version of Viagra is a mixture of herbs, dried bark, rum, wine and honey, which is then steeped for around a month or even years.

04 Larimar jewelry
The DR's unique pale-blue stone, typically used in jewelry, but also in figurines and other small *objets d'art*.

05 Amber jewelry
Prehistoric stone mined in the DR, primarily in the Northern Cordillera, fashioned into artisanal stone settings.

06 Muñeca sin rostro
Famously produced around the town of Moca, these faceless dolls represent the blend of cultures that make up the Dominican identity and nationhood.

07 Pilon
Wooden mortar and pestle used to crush spices and dishes like *mofongo* (mashed plantains with pork rinds).

08 Chocolate
Pick up some single-origin chocolate bars in the DR, one of the world's larger producers of organic cocoa.

09 Bottle of rum
Known for its smoothness and hearty taste, as well as for being less sweet than its Jamaican counterparts. Dozens of brands are available.

10 Espadrilles
Spanish-style, casual, canvas, flat-soled walking shoes crafted from a boutique shop in the city.

01 AYNA DUSHEMOVA/SHUTTERSTOCK, **02** PZAXE/SHUTTERSTOCK, **03** ANNA FEVRALEVA/SHUTTERSTOCK, **04** NIFOLWIGHT/SHUTTERSTOCK, **05** KIVANDAM/SHUTTERSTOCK, MACIN/SHUTTERSTOCK, **06** GIUSEPPECRIMENI/SHUTTERSTOCK, **07** NASHLW/SHUTTERSTOCK, **08** GUMPANAT/SHUTTERSTOCK, **09** EMKA74/SHUTTERSTOCK, **10** ZHEKOSS/SHUTTERSTOCK

05 HISTORY & Culture Fix

HISTORY | ART | CULTURE

Many travelers to the DR are solely chasing the sun, so indoor explorations of world-class cultural institutions aren't usually on their radar. That's their loss because Santo Domingo's museums showcase contemporary art, early Dominican culture and pivotal historical figures.

DOMINGO LEIVA/GETTY IMAGES

How To

Getting there Line 1 of Santo Domingo's metro stops a few blocks from Plaza de la Cultura.

Break it up In Zona Colonial, a half-dozen restaurants housed in 16th- and 17th-century buildings line the northwest side of Plaza España; nighttime is magical.

Admission Most museums have relatively minimal admission fees (no more than RD$150) and audio guides in English are often available.

DENOVYI/SHUTTERSTOCK

Big-Name House Tours

The list of 15th- to 17th-century historical figures who set foot in the DR is a veritable who's who: Cristóbal Colón (Christopher Columbus), Hernán Cortés, Francisco Pizarro, Juan Ponce de León and Vasco Núñez de Balboa all spent time here. So it's no surprise that Santo Domingo provides plenty of opportunities to peek through a residential window onto history.

'Viceroy of the Indies' Diego Columbus (son of Christopher) and his wife Doña María de Toledo lived in what is now the **Museo Alcázar de Colón** in the early 16th century. Anchoring the northeast corner of Plaza España and designed in a Gothic Mudéjar transitional style, it's been restored several times and displays household pieces and other artifacts from the Columbus family.

BAILEY JOHNSON/LONELY PLANET

The Mystery of the Moving Don

Since his death in Valladolid, Spain in 1506, Christopher Columbus' remains have done their own traveling. Though the DR maintains that the massive Faro a Colón monument (p76) holds the Admiral's bones, DNA testing in 2024 confirmed Spain's claims that his remains lie in Seville.

Left Museo de las Casas Reales (p72) **Top left** Exterior of Museo Alcázar de Colón **Above** View of Plaza España from Museo Alcázar de Colón

The **Museo de las Casas Reales** was the longtime seat of Spanish authority in the Caribbean, housing the governor's office and the powerful Audiencia Real (Royal Court). Built in the Renaissance style during the 16th century, it showcases colonial-period objects, including treasures recovered from sunken Spanish galleons.

Fast-forward several centuries and historical periods later: one of the best places to grasp Dominican pride and its origins and to understand the country's early years is the **Museo Casa Duarte** (aka Instituto Duartiano), which celebrates the life of Juan Pablo Duarte. Widely regarded as the father of Dominican independence, Duarte, along with followers of his underground separatist movement, captured Santo Domingo from Haiti, which controlled a united Hispaniola at that time, in a bloodless coup. Inside, wax figures, artifacts and photos tell the story.

Other Museums of Note

Museo Bellapart Incongruously located on the 5th floor of a large Honda dealership is this significant private collection of Dominican painting and sculpture.

Museo del Ron y la Caña Housed in a restored 16th-century building, exhibits here celebrate rum and sugarcane. At the bar you can sample the wares.

Museo Casa de Tostado Beautifully restored 16th-century home of writer Francisco Tostado with displays of restored 19th-century furnishings and household objects.

Amber World Museum The place to grasp the global significance of amber with sophisticated exhibits explaining (in Spanish and English) its origins and the Dominican mining processes.

Plaza de la Cultura

The **Plaza de la Cultura**, a large, centrally located, sun-baked park, is a one-stop location to get your bearings on Dominican art and indigenous culture. The area, once owned by the dictator Trujillo and later 'donated' to the public after his assassination in 1961, also contains the national theater and library. To familiarize yourself with the DR's best-known modern artists, including Luís Desangles, Adriana Billini, Celeste Woss y Gil, José Vela Zanetti, Dario Suro and Martín Santos, browse the galleries of the **Museo de Arte Moderno**. Inventive and fresh temporary exhibitions run the installation and multimedia route.

More old-fashioned, even dusty, but worthwhile nevertheless is the **Museo del Hombre Dominicano**, with its collection of Taíno artifacts, including stone axes and intriguing urns and carvings. Other exhibits focus on Carnival, slavery and the colonial period, African influences in the DR (including a small section on Vodou) and contemporary rural Dominican life. The plaza is also home to a museum dedicated to the natural world, but this is dated and can be missed.

Left Museo de Arte Moderno
Below Museo del Hombre Dominicano

FROM LEFT: JORGE RODRIGUEZ - JARS MCLUCIEN/GETTY IMAGES, JOHN MITCHELL/ALAMY

Listings

BEST OF THE REST

Fiestas

Carnival

The best of Dominican music, dance, art and street food converge in a costumed spectacle in February that outshines the festivities elsewhere in the country.

International Book Festival

Santo Domingo's longstanding celebration of literature is the largest and most important book fair in the Caribbean. The event often includes another country as a guest of honor and celebrates the work of a specific domestic writer.

Merengue Festival

The largest in the country, this two-week celebration of merengue, *bachata,* salsa, Caribbean rhythms, reggaeton and reggae is held yearly. Most of the activity is on the Malecón.

¡Salud!

Cultura Cervecera

Refuge for hopheads both Dominican and foreign, this is one of the city's best bets to escape the Presidente stranglehold. There are nearly 150 craft beers by the bottle.

El Sartén

A mix of *capitaleños* (Santo Domingo residents) get down to *son, bachata* and merengue at this old-school space.

Proud Mary Art Bar

This chill spot is one of the oldest bars in the Zona Colonial, defined by its exotic lamps, killer sangria and live music.

Parada 77

This laid-back, grungy place with graffiti-covered walls serves up strong sangria and a merengue soundtrack. The vibe becomes decidedly high-energy on Sunday nights.

El Patio

Small, beautiful space mixing top-flight cocktails in the bar of the new Kimpton Las Mercedes Hotel.

Sugarcane, La Casa del Ron

Sip strong, if pricey, rum-based cocktails on this 3rd-floor rooftop tasting terrace (with tables made from rum barrels) directly across the street from the oldest still-standing cathedral in the Americas.

Favorite Fine Dining

La Cocina de Cheska $$

Travelers might stick out at this locals-only chef-run Spanish tapas spot with tables on the Parque Arturo Pellerano Castro, a charming cobblestone plaza at the southeastern tip of the Zona Colonial.

Puerta del Conde (p76)

SANTO DOMINGO REVIEWS

Buche Perico $$$

One of the city's more spectacular dining rooms, with light streaming through the greenhouse-like ceiling several stories above. The quality of the service and food is no less impressive: dishes include seared raw tuna and goat risotto.

Pat'e Palo $$$

The most happening and deservedly longest-surviving of Plaza España's restaurant row with a menu including creatively designed dishes such as Angus beef carpaccio in truffle oil and mushrooms.

Trattoria Angiolino $$$

Small and casually sophisticated, this old-school family-owned trattoria serves up large portions of delicious pasta (such as pasta osso buco) and hefty steaks (such as the 1.4kg sirloin), good for two or three people.

Laurel SD $$$

Fine-dining DR-style with a massive wine room and menu of creatively designed dishes mixing Asian, Dominican and North American influences.

Mitre Restaurant & Wine Bar $$$

Sleek restaurant in an upscale business and residential district serving a creative and eclectic fusion of Asian, Italian and Dominican cuisines. The upstairs wine and cigar bar are more casual.

Casual, Quick Eats

Paletas Bajo Cero $

The display of popsicles at this small shop is nearly as aesthetically pleasing as it is appetizing, with row after row of multihued natural fruit flavors and colors.

Barra Payán $

Capitaleños have been lining up for this fast-food joint's delicious signature pork sandwich

ORLANDO BARRÍA/EPA-EFE/SHUTTERSTOCK/SHUTTERSTOCK

Jenny Polanco (p76)

(as well as burgers) before and after late nights out since the 1950s.

D'Luis Parrillada $$

This open-air restaurant perched over the ocean just a few blocks from the Zona Colonial has a large menu ranging from fajitas, grilled and barbecue meats to sandwiches and seafood.

Detroit Pizza RD $$

Possibly the capital's best pizza and the desserts aren't too shabby either. In Piantini.

Boutique Specialty Shops

La Alpargatería

Workshop and store for a growing brand with an international clientele. Painstakingly handcrafted artisanal espadrilles created by fourth-generation shoemakers.

Caoba Cigars

Small shop selling cigars; staff members will explain the cigar-making process from start to finish.

Galería Bolós

Stylish furniture made from recycled wood collected around the Zona Colonial and beyond, displayed alongside avant-garde art sourced across the DR and Haiti.

Galería de Arte María del Carmen

Long running art gallery showcasing a wide range of talented Dominican painters. Opening hours variable.

Jenny Polanco

An iconic Dominican womenswear designer who perfectly blends modern elegance with Caribbean roots. Plus jewelry and bags, all with a flair.

Serigrafia Artistica

Print shop with local art operating since the 1960s. Owner Alfredo is up for a chat.

Monuments & Buildings

Altar de la Patria

This marble mausoleum holds the remains of three national heroes: Juan Pablo Duarte, Francisco del Rosario Sánchez and Ramón Matías Mella.

Capilla de la Tercera Orden Dominica

With a graceful baroque facade, the building now used by the office of the archbishop was built in 1729 and is the only colonial structure in Santo Domingo that remains fully intact.

Casa de Francia

Now housing the French embassy, this marvel of masonry built in the early 16th century was originally home to Hernán Cortés. Check out its facade; visitors aren't permitted past the lobby.

Faro a Colón

Resembling a cross between a Soviet-era apartment block and a Las Vegas–style ancient Mayan ruin, this massive monument purports to contain Columbus' remains.

Reloj del Sol

This sundial was built in 1753 and positioned so that officials in the Royal Houses could see the time with only a glance from their eastern windows; it remains accurate today.

Puerta del Conde

It was atop this gate that the very first Dominican flag was raised and still stands as the supreme symbol of Dominican patriotism.

Dominicaness Is on the Menu

Villar Hermanos $

Occupying almost an entire city block, Villar Hermanos has two parts: a bustling diner serving classic Dominican cafeteria food and hot grilled sandwiches, and an outdoor garden restaurant with a slightly more upscale menu.

Adrian Tropical $

This popular family-friendly chain with a spectacular location overlooking the Caribbean doles out Dominican specialties such as *mofongo* as well as standard meat dishes. An inexpensive buffet is an option.

La Cafetera Colonial $

Opened in 1932, this long, narrow greasy spoon is still catering to a regular clientele for strong espressos, and burgers and such.

Mesón D'Bari $

Popular with tourists and sophisticated *capitaleños* on weekends, Mesón D'Bari occupies

Capilla de la Tercera Orden Dominica

a charmingly decaying colonial home with a menu of Dominican (and a few international) dishes. There's live music on some weekend nights.

Jalao $$

A towering and cavernous restaurant brimming with Dominican style, Jalao is over-the-top theme-park touristy but attracts local crowds, too. Live music and pricey, if adventurous, food.

El Conuco $$

Dominicans as well as tour groups come here to get traditionally prepared dishes while taking in merengue and *bachata* performances in a *palapa* (palm leaf)-topped dining room covered with traditional decorations.

La Dolce Vita Cafe Spots

Cafeteria El Conde de Peñalba

Ideal for people-watching with a commanding location at the busiest corner of the Zona Colonial.

Segazona Cafe

Popular with tourists and Dominicans alike for its prime piece of cobblestone real estate, Segazona is good for an espresso drink or cocktail and Italian food.

PAUL KIM/ALAMY

Cafeteria El Conde de Peñalba

Corner Coffee Shop

Serene, with tables spilling out onto a picturesque cobblestone lane, this place is good for a cappuccino, a glass of wine or a sweet pastry.

Mamey Librería Café

Featuring stone courtyards, a fountain with a flowering trinitaria and vertical gardens, the space is ideal for relaxing with a book or grabbing a drink with friends.

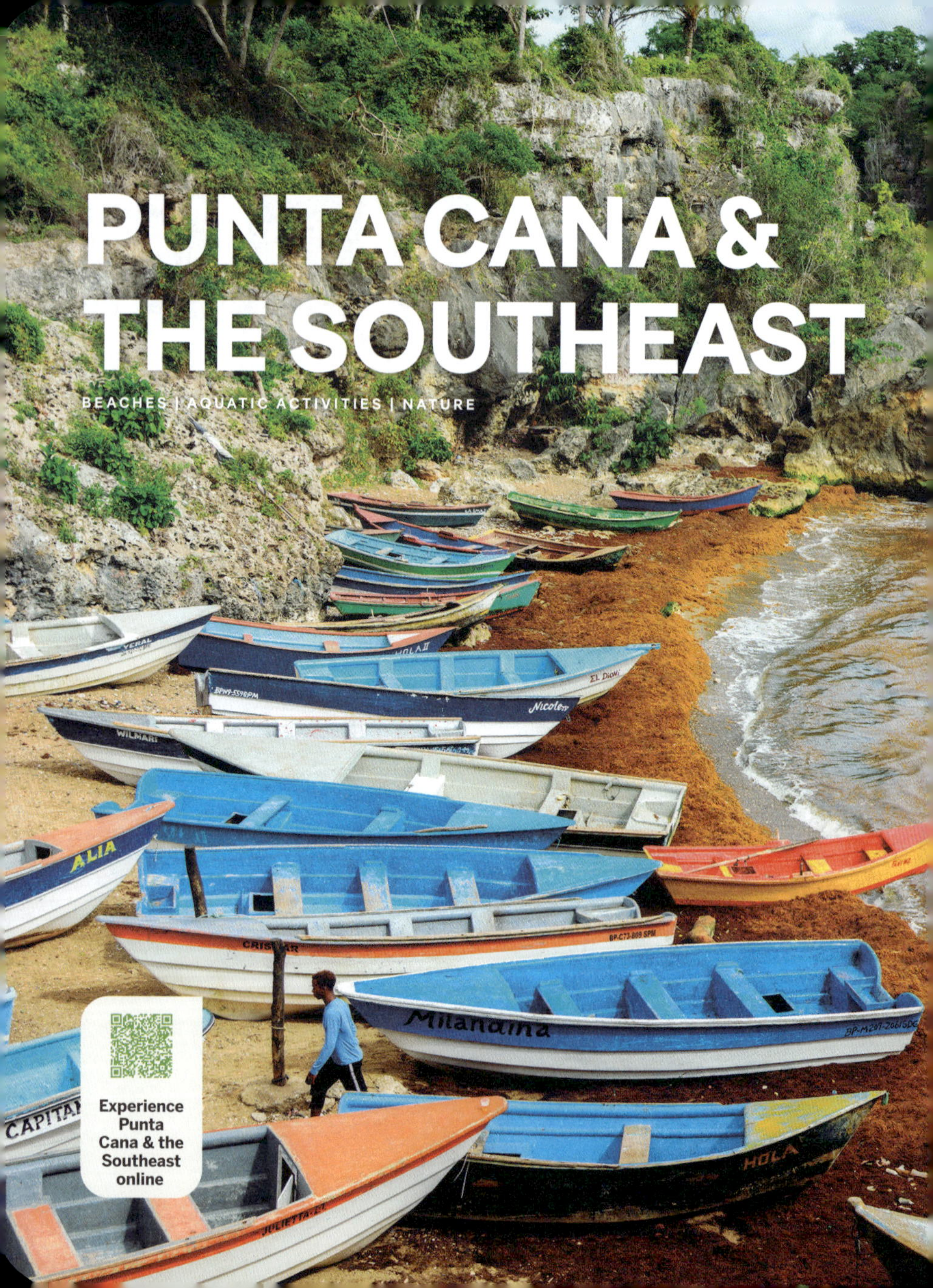
PUNTA CANA & THE SOUTHEAST
BEACHES | AQUATIC ACTIVITIES | NATURE
Experience Punta Cana & the Southeast online

Kayak mangrove lagoons through **Parque Nacional Los Haitises** (p84)

2½hr from Punta Cana

Explore ancient underground worlds at **Cueva de las Maravillas** (p86)

25min from La Romana

PUNTA CANA & THE SOUTHEAST

Trip Builder

There's a reason the DR's southeast has become synonymous with Caribbean-style, jumbo-sized, all-inclusive resorts, but there's more to this region than the seemingly endless kilometers of resort-backed beaches. Ditch the crowds to explore hidden caves, bird-filled mangroves and lagoons of crystal-clear water.

Take advantage of, well, nearly everything and anything on offer at sprawling and decadent **Hard Rock Hotel Punta Cana** (p102)

10min from downtown Bávaro

Binge on beaches like the pristine resort-backed **Playa Arena Gorda** around Punta Cana (p97)

10min from downtown Bávaro

Plunge into hidden freshwater lagoons in **Ojos Indígenas Ecological Park** (p105)

10min from Punta Cana

Dine on seafood at pavilion-style restaurants with ocean views in out-of-the-way **Boca de Yuma** (p95)

1hr from Punta Cana

Practicalities

PASCAL HUOT/SHUTTERSTOCK

ARRIVING

Aeropuerto Internacional Punta Cana At the far eastern tip of the island, around 11km south of downtown Punta Cana, the DR's largest and busiest airport is chaotic, with lots of solicitation from drivers on exit. Arrange transfers in advance. Taxis to area resorts average US$35 to US$50.

La Romana International Airport Casa de Campo Handles some direct US flights, as well as charters, primarily servicing Casa de Campo.

HOW MUCH FOR A

Isla Saona trip US$65

Whole fried fish RD$700

Round of golf US$160

GETTING AROUND

Uber and inRide There's no shortage of taxi stands; however, rideshare app prices are much cheaper.

Motoconcho Motorcycle taxis congregate around Plaza Punta Cana in Bávaro and along the beach road in El Cortecito. You can generally find one or two parked at the entrance of most resorts. Fares average RD$100 to RD$200 within the El Cortecito/Bávaro area.

Guagua Local buses start at the main bus terminal, passing all the outdoor malls on the way to El Cortecito, then head down the coastal road past the large hotels to Cruce de Cocoloco, where they turn around and return. Costs depend on distance. They generally pass every 30 minutes between 5am and 8pm.

WHEN TO GO

JAN–MAR
Crowded over holidays and during the North American spring break.

APR–JUN
Showers are a possibility, though they are generally short; hot daytime temps.

JUL–SEP
Seaweed season impact varies from beach to beach.

OCT–DEC
October, post-hurricane, pre-holidays, is great for the budget-conscious.

TOP: BHOFACK2/GETTY IMAGES
BOTTOM: FOTOADICTA/SHUTTERSTOCK

EATING & DRINKING

Punta Cana offers the biggest and most sophisticated selection of restaurants in the DR. You'll find every imaginable international fare at the all-inclusive resorts, while Bávaro and the surrounding region offers a diversity of independent dining. Of course, Dominican food, especially tantalizingly fresh *pescado* (fish), *langosta* (lobster), *lambí* (conch) and *camarones* (shrimp), is everywhere, but it always tastes better on a beach. It's normally prepared on the grill and accompanied by *tostones* (smashed, fried plantains) and/or *moro* (rice and beans).

Don't-miss *morir sonañdo*
Huracan Café (p107)

Best ceviche
Restaurante Playa Blanca (p106)

CONNECT & FIND YOUR WAY

Wi-fi Resort networks range from notoriously inconsistent to poor. If a high-speed connection is paramount for work, consider a VPN.

Navigation Daytime traffic can get gridlocked between the resorts clustered just north of Bávaro and El Cortecito. Renting a car for a day or two is recommended if you prefer to see the surrounding area independently. Major international car-rental agencies are located at the airport.

WHERE TO STAY

All-inclusive resorts of all shapes and sizes are the rule, but there are a smattering of independent lodgings. Pay attention to proximity to the beach.

Neighborhood	Pros/Cons
Bávaro	Some independent choices away from the beach; highest concentration of hotels along beach. Quality can be hit or miss.
Cap Cana	Luxury options; relatively uncongested. Far from non-resort eating options.
Corales & El Cortecito	Walkable, bustling with loads of restaurants and bars. Not for families.
Punta Cana	Quality beaches; lots of choices; close to airport. Fewer independent restaurants.
Bayahibe	Town proper has affordable options; close to restaurants, bars. Beach isn't as good as those nearby.

MEDICAL SERVICES

All-inclusive resorts have small on-site clinics and medical staff who can provide first aid. There are several good private hospitals in the area for more serious issues.

MONEY

Use ATMs at banks or inside malls. Avoid brandless ATMs and those on the street or outside small shops (credit card cloning is a potential danger).

06 KAYAK
Los Haitises

BIRDLIFE | PICTOGRAPHS | NATURE

Parque Nacional Los Haitises boasts the country's highest density and variety of flora and fauna, plus pre-Columbian cave pictographs and green mangrove waters where manatees feed. The most direct, if less used, access is via a kayak tour from Sabana de la Mar, the Southeast's end-of-road town. Avoid big boat groups and take advantage of the area's serenity.

RAFAEL MARTIN-GAITERO/SHUTTERSTOCK

How To

When to go Dry season, from December to April.

Getting there The majority of travelers visit on a half-day trip from Peninsula de Samaná (30 to 40 minutes by boat) or a full-day trip from Punta Cana (2½-hour van or truck trip each way). Both will travel through the mangroves in motorboats of varying sizes.

Soak it up The Río Jivales, which runs through the quirky, rustic and comfortable Paraíso Caño Hondo, has been channeled into 12 magical waterfall-fed pools, perfect for a soak any time of the day.

MAURITIUS IMAGES GMBH/ALAMY

MAURITIUS IMAGES GMBH/ALAMY

Far left bottom Paraíso Caño Hondo **Far left top** Parque Nacional Los Haitises **Left** Kayaking in Parque Nacional Los Haitises

Known as 'land of the mountains,' Parque Nacional Los Haitises encompasses 1375 sq km at the southwestern end of the Bahía de Samaná. It does indeed contain scores of lush hills, jutting some 30m to 50m from the water and coastal wetlands. The area receives a tremendous amount of rainfall (over 2m a year), creating perfect conditions for subtropical humid forest plants such as bamboo, ferns and bromeliads. In fact, Los Haitises contains over 700 species of flora, including four types of mangrove, making it one of the most highly biodiverse regions in the Caribbean.

On the water Gliding smoothly in a kayak through the park's mangrove channels early in the morning is the best opportunity for birders: keep an eye out for brown pelicans, American frigate birds, blue and snow herons, roseate terns, northern jacanas and West Indian whistling ducks. If you're lucky, you may spot the rare Hispaniolan parakeet, notable for its light-green and red feathers, or a manatee feeding in shallow waters by the shore. Typically, kayakers leave at low tide and return at high tide, and are out in relatively open bay water for around 45 minutes of paddling. Vistas get wider and the rocky outcroppings are equally picturesque.

Caves Los Haitises contains a number of limestone caves, some containing intriguing Taíno **pictographs**. Drawn by the native inhabitants of Hispaniola using mangrove shoots, the pictures depict faces, hunting scenes, whales and other shamanistic creatures. Several petroglyphs thought to represent divine guardians are at cave entrances.

Booking Your Tour

The most intimate way to see Parque Nacional Los Haitises is on a kayak excursion booked through **Paraíso Caño Hondo** (paraisocanohondo.com), a one-of-a-kind lodge outside Sabana de la Mar. Several boat operators mill about the park's entrance and generally charge RD$3000 for two people for a 2½-hour tour that typically takes in the mangroves, Bahía de San Lorenzo, Muelle Antigua and Cuevas de la Arena. It's theoretically possible, although unusual, for kayak tours to reach all the way to Cueva de la Línea, one of the largest, most visited (on boat tours) caves for its pictographs. Some tour companies out of Las Terrenas or Punta Cana might be able to arrange these trips as intermediaries.

07 Underground GALLERIES

SPELUNKING | CULTURE | HISTORY

Evidence of Hispaniola's rich history has been written onto the island's landscape, most notably through the thousands of pictographs and petroglyphs painted and carved on the walls of Cueva de las Maravillas by Arawak peoples and Taínos, whose cultures once prospered on the island.

DIANNA TATKOW/SHUTTERSTOCK

How To

Admission Tours of Cueva de las Maravillas run every 25 minutes and cost RD$300/100 for adults/children under 12.

Getting there Cueva de las Maravillas is right on the southeast's major highway. Tour companies generally don't offer trips to other spots; ask locals for directions.

What to wear Shoes (not flip-flops) as cave floors can be wet and slippery and explorations might involve some scrambling.

DANU WIDJAJANTO/WIKIMEDIA/CC BY-SA 4.0

Ancient Archaeology

The most developed of the caves, **Cueva de las Maravillas** resembles a well-lit underground museum and sits just outside the city of La Romana. You can purchase your tickets for the guided tour directly at the cave (cheaper than online). After descending about 25m, you'll navigate through a 250m trail with 10 petroglyphs (rock carvings) and more than 500 pictographs (cave paintings) that depict life among the Taínos through images of people, animals and plants. One room, aptly named the **Water Mirror Gallery**, utilizes an artificial lake to mirror the ceiling of the cave with a pictograph of what appears to be a funeral ritual.

Along the way, you may also spot a few snakes, diplopods, toads and bats among the rocks. But despite the occasional large

DIANNA TATKOW/SHUTTERSTOCK

Taíno Religious Art

The complexity of the Taíno cosmological, religious and spiritual belief systems is displayed for all to see. Petroglyphs representing various deities (sun, moon, earth, rain, fertility, etc) are found all over the Dominican Republic. You just need to know how to read the carvings on the walls.

Bottom left Descent into Cueva de las Maravillas **Top left** Cueva de las Maravillas **Above** Taíno pictographs, Cueva de las Maravillas

marine iguana wandering along the path, the experience doesn't feel 'all-natural' due to the labyrinth of hedges at the entrance and the paved and finished floor through much of the cave system. That being said, it's one of the few experiences in the Dominican Republic accessible to wheelchair and mobility-aid users and strollers, thanks to its ramps and elevator. Keep an eye out for the remarkably long tree roots extending deep into the caves from above, searching for water.

Cueva del Puente

Parque Nacional Cotubanamá has more than 400 caves, many of which contain Taíno pictographs and petroglyphs. The most easily visited is **Cueva del Puente**, where sunlight streams like a laser through an opening in the ceiling; nevertheless, bring a flashlight, as cell phone ones aren't generally strong enough. There are a number of pictograms depicting animals and humanlike figures that might represent Taíno deities. It's a 3km walk from

Other Taíno Sites

Los Tres Ojos A popular spot east of the Río Ozama in Santo Domingo, consisting of three humid caverns with dark-blue lagoons connected by stalactite-filled passages. A long stairway down a narrow tunnel and a path at the bottom leads through the caves, where Taíno artifacts have been found.

Museo Arqueológico Regional Altos de Chavon Part of the gated complex just outside La Romana with one of the most extensive collections of Taíno artifacts.

Reserva Antropológica Cuevas del Pomier Like reading a history written in stone, this is one of the most extensive prehistoric cave art sites in the Caribbean. It's 10km north of central San Cristóbal.

the Guaraguao park entrance (signage is almost non-existent once you're on your way).

Cueva de Berna

Several kilometers west of Boca de Yuma on the way to the entrance of Parque Nacional Cotubanamá is **Cueva de Berna** (aka Bernard, named for one of the first non-indigenous fishers to settle here in the late 19th century). There is normally a caretaker sitting outside the entrance who can accompany you up the rickety ladder and deep into the cave to take a look at scattered Taíno pictograms; a small gratuity is appreciated. There's usually enough sunlight streaming in through an opening in the roof to see unaided, and bats and even owls might flit about.

Left Cueva del Puente
Below Cueva de Berna

FROM LEFT: ILYAS KALIMULLIN/SHUTTERSTOCK, HACKENBERG-PHOTO-COLOGNE/ALAMY

Hispaniola's First Peoples

DISCOVERIES ABOUT THE ISLAND'S ANCIENT CIVILIZATIONS CONTINUE

Hispaniola had been inhabited for more than three millennia by the time Christopher Columbus landed on the island in 1492, but it was the Taíno ('the friendly people') who prospered for around 700 years, until Columbus' 'discovery' brought their ultimate downfall.

PRINT COLLECTOR/GETTY IMAGES

Left Engraving of Christopher Colombus, arriving on what would later be called Hispaniola, by Theodor de Bry (1590) **Center** Taíno bowl dating from the 13th to 15th centuries **Right** *Casabe* bread

Ancient Remnants

Some of the earliest evidence of human habitation on Hispaniola (stone-flaked tools and the like) dates all the way back to 4000 BCE. Originally thought to have been brought by hunter-gatherers migrating from the Yucatán Peninsula in Mexico, recent archaeological discoveries have cast doubt on this theory: a rare and significant find dubbed 'El Pozito,' consisting of sophisticated stone tools such as axes and pestles, was made by an Italian-Dominican team of archaeologists on the Samaná peninsula in 2021. The site's fairly isolated, protected location in the country's northeast gave rise to speculation that the makers of these tools might have arrived from Puerto Rico, on an exploration themselves. Importantly, it's thought these people were genetically distinct from later arrivals, such as the Taíno ancestors, the Arawaks.

The Next Wave

It wasn't until around 1200 BCE that ancestral Arawaks are thought to have arrived in Hispaniola, via the Lesser Antilles. Dubbed the 'Saladoid culture,' they lived in settled agricultural communities and are best known for their sophisticated pottery. A third wave of migrants arrived in Hispaniola between 500 CE and 1000 CE, with the rich seafaring culture of the Taíno, and the population expanded rapidly – the total at the time of Columbus' arrival was around 500,000. These farmers lived in 'districts' and villages of 1000 to 2000 people, organized in chiefdoms called *caciques*. Comparatively little of pre-colonization Taíno culture has survived to the modern age. Pottery and stone tools form the most common artifacts, along with jewelry of

SEPIA TIMES/GETTY IMAGES

BRIAN YARVIN/SHUTTERSTOCK

bone, shell and gold that was panned from rivers. Clothing was made of cotton or pounded bark fibers. Though Taíno artifacts are relatively few, the crops they introduced to the world were revolutionary, from tobacco to yams, cassava and pineapples.

The Beginning of the End

In 1492 Christopher Columbus set sail from Spain with 90 men in the *Pinta*, the *Niña* and the *Santa María* bound for Asia. He sailed west rather than east, expecting to circumnavigate the globe, and instead 'discovered' the 'New World' for the 'Old.' After stops at the small Bahamian island of Guanahaní and present-day Cuba (which Columbus initially mistook for Japan), a mountainous landscape appeared before the sailors. Columbus named it 'La Isla Española' or 'the Spanish Island,' which was later corrupted to 'Hispaniola.' He made landfall at Môle St-Nicholas in what is now known as Haiti on December 7, and days later ran the *Santa María* onto a reef. Here, on Christmas Day, he established Villa La Navidad, the first European settlement in the Americas.

> A third wave of migrants arrived in Hispaniola between 500 CE and 1000 CE, with the rich seafaring culture of the Taínos.

Columbus was greeted with great warmth by the Taínos, who offered him gifts of gold jewelry. Capturing a handful of Taínos to impress his royal patrons, Columbus sailed back to Spain to be showered with glory. He returned within a year, leading 17 ships of soldiers and colonists.

Food Legacy

A common thread from ancient Taíno cooking fires to upscale Santo Domingo bistros is a starchy bread known as *casabe*. Low in fat and high in carbs, it's made from the ground roots of the cassava (aka manioc; related to yucca), which was once a principal crop of the Taíno and other indigenous peoples throughout the Caribbean and South America, in part because it grew quickly and was easy to plant. It was later spread by Europeans to their colonies in Africa and Asia. Fairly tasteless by itself, *casabe* is best served with butter, salt, tomato or avocado, or alongside traditional soups and stews, where it can be used to soak up excess liquid.

In his absence, La Navidad had been razed by the Taínos in reprisal for the kidnapping of their people by the colonizers, so Columbus sailed east and established La Isabela, named for Spain's queen, on the north coast of the DR; the first church in the Americas was erected here. However, La Isabela was plagued with disease, and within five years the capital of the new colony was moved to Santo Domingo, where it has remained.

> The Spanish continued to break up Taíno villages, kill their chiefs and put the entire population to work for the colonizers.

The Collapse

Columbus' early administration was a disaster and the appointment of his brother Bartholomé proved no better. Their haphazard rule soon had the colonists up in arms and a replacement sent from Spain returned the brothers home in chains. The colony would now be run with military harshness.

The Taínos bore the brunt of this. In 1503, Queen Anacaona of the Taíno kingdom of Xaragua in central Hispaniola was arrested by the Spanish governor and publicly executed, effectively marking the end of Taíno independence on the island. The people were already stricken by European illnesses that sent their numbers crashing; on top of this, Spain introduced *encomienda,* forced labor requiring the Taíno to dig up quotas of gold. Enriquillo, a Taíno *cacique,* led a rebellion against the Spanish in the Bahoruco mountains near the present-day DR–Haiti border, which lasted from 1519 to 1533. But the Spanish continued to break up Taíno villages, kill their chiefs and put the entire population to work for the colonizers. Within three decades of their first meeting with Europeans, the Taínos were reduced to a shadow of their previous numbers.

As the Taíno civilization collapsed, so did the gold mines, and no number of imported African slaves could make up the shortfall. Spain dropped Hispaniola as quickly as it had found it, turning its attention instead to the immense riches coming from its new possessions in Mexico and Peru. Santo Domingo was reduced to a trading post for gold and silver convoys, but with the opening of new trade routes via Cuba, it couldn't even hold onto that position. After the English privateer Sir Francis Drake sacked Santo Domingo in 1586, it was effectively abandoned for 50 years, further signaling the decline of Spanish Hispaniola.

POWEROFFOREVER/GETTY IMAGES

POWEROFFOREVER/GETTY IMAGES

SAATON/SHUTTERSTOCK

UNIVERSAL HISTORY ARCHIVE/GETTY IMAGES

Living Legacy

The lasting influence and survival of Taíno identity and cultural practices isn't so readily visible in urban parts of the DR. But in rural areas – for example, the El Valle area on Samaná – it's more marked as oral traditions and cosmological beliefs have been passed down through the generations. Musically, however, you can see and hear Taíno sounds everywhere. The *güira*, a percussive musical instrument used to infuse merengue and *bachata* songs with a rhythmical rasping sound, was originally adopted by the Taínos who employed dried, hollowed-out gourds and a forked stick to produce music for their *areítos* (ceremonial songs). Today the *güira* has been modernized – but not by much. Instead of using vegetables, the modern *güira* is made of latten brass; it typically looks like a cylindrical cheese grater that is scraped with a long metal pick. The rasping sound is essentially the same – the modern-day instrument just lasts a little longer.

The shells of conch, a mollusk served up all over in Dominican restaurants, were used by the Arawaks and Taínos in tool-making, and carved into fine necklaces and other jewelry (today, you can find jewelry with conch shapes made from Larimar sold in the DR). Taínos also used ground conch shell as an ingredient for a hallucinogenic powder in religious ceremonies. Centuries later, blowing the conch became the emblematic call to arms of the Haitian slave rebellion, and is still commemorated in that country's popular art.

Literary History

The Dominican Republic's literary history dates to the Spanish colonial period (1492–1795). It was then that Bartolomé de Las Casas, a Spanish friar, recorded the early history of the Caribbean and pleaded for fair treatment of the Taínos in *Historia de las Indias (History of the Indies).*

Gastón Fernando Deligne Pérez' *Fantasías Indíginas (Indian Fantasies)*, imagines encounters between Spanish conquistadores and the Taíno, while Gonzalo Fernández de Oviedo's *La Historia General y Natural de las Indias* (1526) traces Spain's colonization of the Americas, as well as its flora and fauna, through first-hand experience and interviews.

Far left A 19th-century etching of Bartholomé Columbus burning a Taíno village and killing the people **Left** A 19th-century etching of Taíno defending themselves against the Spanish conquistadores **Top left** *Güira* **Top right** Oviedo's *La Historia General y Natural de las Indias* (1526)

08 End-of-Road FEASTS

FOOD | VIEWS | CULTURE

Away from the coastline colonized by resorts the size of city states, there are oceanfront villages where moored fishing boats line the waterfront and locals dig into bounteous plates of seafood. After sunset, when the tourist rush hour has abated, they're transformed into oceanside oases.

LENA SERDITOVA/SHUTTERSTOCK

How To

Getting around Renting a car is the way to go and roadways throughout are mostly paved. Drive extra cautiously at night. Or Uber it.

When to go Afternoons, with time to enjoy some sun before watching it dip beyond the horizon.

Ponce de León The Spanish explorer had a house built near Boca de Yuma when he governed the nearby town of Higüey for the Spanish Crown.

HACKENBERG-PHOTO-COLOGNE/ALAMY

Bottom left Beachside restaurant, Boca de Yuma **Top left** Playa Bayahibe

Bayahibe Originally founded by fishers from Puerto Rico, Bayahibe, 22km east of La Romana, is a tranquil beach village except when operating as a jumping-off point for boats bound for Isla Saona. Just to the north and several kilometers south in the beachfront enclave of **Dominicus Americanus** are loads of high-end accommodations. Most guests stay on or near their accommodations at night. But you're bound for a more subdued and romantic evening if you head to **Mare Nuestro** and its breezy 2nd-story patio overlooking the harborfront. Nearby, several bars occupy a spot on the mainland side of a little peninsula jutting out into the sea.

Boca de Yuma The ramshackle little town of Boca de Yuma, situated at the literal end-of-the-road, makes for a great little getaway. Rough, unpaved roads and half-finished buildings lead to a quiet seaside promontory where waves crash dramatically into the rocky shore. Several old-fashioned **pavilion-style restaurants**, with spectacular ocean views, line the road overlooking the ocean; all focus on fresh seafood.

Miches Nearly a decade ago, the road north from Bávaro was paved all the way to Miches, on the southern shore of the Bahía de Samaná. No longer isolated, and fairly picturesque when seen from the surrounding hills, it's still an ordinary-looking town. **Playa Miches**, just east of the town proper, is a long and wide beach not especially good for swimming, but good for a sand-in-the-toes meal. Several restaurants concentrated along the seafront are pleasant places for meals with views.

Dive Destinations

Bayahibe is widely regarded as one of the best scuba-diving destinations in the country, with around 20 sites, including an 85m ship wreck and a 290m tunnel flooded with freshwater in **Parque Nacional del Este** (only for advanced divers). Another top site, ominously called **Shark Point**, is the wreck of a massive 89m cargo ship near Isla Catalina. Only 40km east of Santo Domingo, **Boca Chica** has another two dozen sites. The most recommended are the two shipwrecks: the 39m-long *Hickory* and the 33m-long *Catuan*, found in the La Caleta underwater preserve.

09 BEACH Bumming It

SAND | WATER SPORTS | ROAD TRIPS

Sun, sea and sand – this trifecta sums up the country's eastern seaboard. Courageously brave sunburn and heatstroke in search of your ideal. There's more than enough to go around for every day-tripper to find their own perfect piece of real estate.

PHOTOPIXEL/SHUTTERSTOCK

How To

When to go Year-round, although September and October receive the most rain, with periodic short-lasting showers, and November is the most humid.

Getting around Rent a motorbike if exploring nearby; otherwise, a rental car gives you the most flexibility. International car-rental agencies are located at the airport; some have offices scattered elsewhere in the area.

Bird's-eye views Get lifted by a crane to dine 46m (150ft) up at **Dinner in the Sky** in Punta Cana for panoramic views.

Classic Caribbean Coastline

Ten or so beaches fall under the Punta Cana umbrella, stretching across more than 50km of coastline. Theoretically, you can stroll from less-exclusive stretches to nicer spots in front of resorts – but without the proper color wrist bracelet you won't be able to get a towel or chair.

Stretches of Bávaro's main beach, **Playa El Cortecito** (to the north) and **Los Corales** (to the south) feel like an extension of the bustling, walkable 'downtown' Bávaro; the former, in particular, tends to be crowded with vendors.

North of El Cortecito is **Playa Arena Gorda**, lined with all-inclusive resorts and their guests on banana boats, parasailing or just soaking in the sun. A further 9km north is the best accessible surf beach, **Playa del Macao**,

PHOTOPIXEL/SHUTTERSTOCK

Left Stretch of Bávaro beach
Top left Playa Arena Gorda

a gorgeous stretch of sand best reached by car. Surf schools with board rentals are plentiful. It's also a stop-off for a slew of ATV (all-terrain vehicle) tours that tear up and down the beach every day – there's less noise at the far northern end of the beach. The golden sands of **Playa Uvero Alto**, the area's northernmost beach, are 10km further north. It's worth noting that waves here are more Atlantic-like than Caribbean: undertow and currents can impact swimming and seaweed can blanket non-resort parts of the beach.

In the other direction, south of Bávaro and El Cortecito, is **Playa Cabo Engaño**, an isolated beach that you'll need a vehicle, preferably a 4WD, to reach. And then there's the furthest southern beach, the gorgeous, snaking stunner **Playa Juanillo**, whose sands are cleaned daily by Cap Cana staff – just maybe the fairest of them all!

Sugar, Please

It wasn't until the mid-19th century, when prosperous Cuban plantation owners began to seek out new territory, that a sugar industry took root in the DR. But it was the first steam-powered sugar mill *(ingenio)* opened in 1879 near **San Pedro de Macorís** that jump-started things. This commercial port town was soon booming, with more than a half-dozen modern plants in operation by 1920. San Pedro, later synonymous with baseball, became an elegant and cosmopolitan town known for its poets and sugar wealth. When the European sugar industry was destroyed by WWI, Caribbean suppliers stepped in. Sugar became the DR's leading export and the US its leading buyer.

Beach Access

By law, every beachy shoreline is open to the public. However, two of the best, Playa Blanca (inside Punta Cana Resorts) and Playa Juanillo operate as de facto private beaches requiring an admission fee. Juanillo, part of the Cap Cana development, costs US$50. However, the money 'goes toward' food and drinks bought at the excellent beachfront restaurant.

FROM LEFT: PASHAPIXEL/GETTY IMAGES, ORIOLE GIN/SHUTTERSTOCK

Mix Things Up

Those motivated to find another flavor of beach can take a day trip further north or east depending on their taste.

Wild, windswept 3km-long **Playa Limón**, beyond the sugar plantations and inland mountains to the north, feels like beaches further south must have many decades ago. Come on a weekday and you might feel like a more fortunate Robinson Crusoe type. A serene lagoon, known as a bird-watching spot, feeds into the ocean on the eastern end of the beach, surrounded by grassy wetlands and mangroves.

Juan Dolio, a beach town only 64km east of Santo Domingo, brings a typically festive Dominican vibe. The relatively narrow public **beach** on the western side of town can get extremely cramped and loud, especially on weekends. The beach area in front of the high-rise condominiums and resorts on the more prosperous eastern side is wider and softer; public access is via a walkway between two condos.

ALEKSANDR RYBALKO/SHUTTERSTOCK

Left Playa del Macao **Top** Horses on Playa Limón **Above** Beachside signpost

10 All-Inclusive RESORTS

BEACHES | POOLS | FOOD

The crown jewel of Dominican tourism, scores of gargantuan resorts that are synonymous with all-you-can-eat buffets and Club Med and cruise ship–like group activities, are deservedly famous for offering carefree, indulgent holidays. From adults-only to cartoon-themed, there's something for everyone.

WORLD POKER TOUR/FLICKR/CC BY-ND 2.0

How To

What's included? Usually breakfast, lunch, dinner, alcohol and use of resort facilities. Activities like golf, snorkeling and off-site excursions cost extra.

When to go From January to May. The priciest period is from Christmas to New Year's.

Tips Bring your own beach equipment and paraphernalia (costs at resorts are exorbitant). Don't walk alone on the beach at night or drink the tap water.

PICTORIAL PRESS LTD/ALAMY

Welcome to the crown jewel of the DR's tourism economy, where buffet items seem to outnumber grains of sand and wading to swim-up pool bars counts as an outing. With the right frame of mind and expectations, all-inclusive resorts can make for a fantastic vacation. And while the majority of guests tend to stay put, there's no shortage of packaged excursions to help you venture further afield if you wish to.

Choosing Your Stay

There's no one-size-fits-all property or location that will satisfy everyone. Some resorts have fantastic beaches, but mediocre food, or vice versa. Others feature spacious, luxurious rooms, but overly crowded pool scenes. These are trivial issues, of course, in the scheme of things. Do your research and pay attention to the fine print, including specifics of location.

PASCAL HUOT/SHUTTERSTOCK

The Lay of the Land

Punta Cana (Gray-Haired Point) refers to the area just east and south of the Punta Cana International Airport, the easternmost tip of the country. However, the majority of resorts are scattered around the beaches of Bávaro, a town whose original raison d'être was to house resort workers.

Left Royalton Punta Cana (p102) **Top left** Eden pool, Hard Rock Hotel Punta Cana (p102) **Above** Excellence Punta Cana (p102)

Many brands have multiple offerings, ranging from budget-minded to luxurious, and expectations and quality can vary wildly. For example, Royalton has three resorts in the area and the **Royalton Punta Cana**, while generic, is on one of the best beaches, whereas the Royalton Chic Punta Cana receives more than its fair share of negative reviews.

The five-star **Majestic Mirage Punta Cana** is known for the high quality of its food; however, it's not on the finest beach. **Lopesan Costa Bávaro** gets accolades for the food and for having one of the finest pools, plus an adults-only area. **Excellence Punta Cana** has one of the longest stretches of beachfront, while **Zoetry Agua Punta Cana**, on the higher end of costs, stands out for its Balinese-style furnishing and relaxing vibe.

Imagine Las Vegas on the Caribbean and you have an idea of the **Hard Rock Hotel Punta Cana**, one of the most well-rounded resorts on one of the best beaches. Rooms,

The Saona Lowdown

It's hard for any particular beach to stand out amidst so much stiff competition. Yet Isla Saona's powdery white-sand and aquamarine gentle surf does. White palm trees that provide shade and you can observe endangered starfish at the bottom of the waist-deep **Blue Lagoon** (most coral has been damaged by heavy boat traffic). This would be perfect if it weren't for the ear-splitting dance music and vendors wandering the beach in search of those in need of hair braiding and shell necklaces. The majority of visitors are ferried to Bayahibe early in the morning from resorts; it can be a long, uncomfortable amount of drive time.

Left Isla Saona **Below** Fishing tour operator, Playa El Cortecito

especially the suites, are fabulous and the interests of every age are satisfied. It's just so, so large.

If you're traveling with friends, keep in mind that resorts discourage day visitors by imposing high day-pass fees (or not allowing them at all), so it's best to stay together.

Activity Menu

Virtually every imaginable water activity, and only slightly fewer land-based ones, are on offer and every resort has a tour desk that can arrange these.

Deep-sea fishing enthusiasts can charter a boat (minimum four people, four hours) for marlin, tuna, wahoo and barracuda, and an enormous number of people head out to the wildly popular Isla Saona. On Playa El Cortecito, local guides offer 2½-hour snorkeling trips and two-hour glass-bottom boat rides to a nearby reef, as well as parasailing, banana-boat riding and the like. There are a few pushy kiosks near the northern end of the beach, although you'll be approached by touts anyway as soon as you set foot in town and on the beach. Keep in mind that the cheaper prices often mean a lack of license or insurance.

On land, there's several highly regarded golf courses, zip-lining, 4WD buggie tours, horseback riding, several nature and animal reserves, and long day trips to Santo Domingo.

11 FORESTED Swimming Holes

FRESHWATER | BIRDLIFE | WALKING

Though development seems to be encroaching on every inch of the Dominican southeastern coastline, areas of pristine coastal plains, mangrove forests and lagoons – some where Taínos once lived – remain to be explored. Take a dip in refreshing river-fed swimming holes deep in the forested shade with birdsong as your soundtrack, far from congested hotel pools.

WENDY GUNDERSON/GETTY IMAGES

How To

Getting there Organized transportation from most resorts can take you to Ojos Indígenas and Scape Park; you'll need your own transportation for Hoyo Claro (4WD rental vehicle or Uber).

Fee Ojos Indígenas is free for those staying at one of the Punta Cana Resort's properties. Otherwise, it's a hefty US$90 for the 2¾-hour tour.

Tip Don't wear sunscreen or bug repellent when taking a dip in the lagoons and swimming holes.

LUCAS INACIO/ALAMY

Bottom left Hoyo Azul
Top left Swimming hole, Ojos Indígenas Ecological Park

Ojos Indígenas Ecological Park Somewhat incongruously situated about 500m south of (and part of) the fairly luxurious Puntacana Resort & Club, Ojos Indígenas Ecological Park covers over 6 sq km of protected coastal and inland habitat and is home to some 100 bird species (27 of which are indigenous species native only to the DR), 160 insect species and 500 plant species. Utilize the park map provided upon admission to find your way along the entirely flat pathway through forested mangroves to the lagoon of your choice. There are 12 in total, but only four are suitable for swimming; the first you come to, **Inriri**, is possibly the best for swimming, and **Cacibajagua** is another option. One of the lagoons, crammed with turtles, is only for observing, well, the turtles.

Scape Park Nestled within the touristy bells and whistles of the nearby Cap Cana area lies the eco-adventure Scape Park, most notably worth visiting for **Hoyo Azul**, a stunning cenote (say-NO-tay) with crystal-clear water, perfect for swimming and snorkeling. You can also explore the park's verdant jungle on a zip-line tour or investigate its caverns and underground caves.

Hoyo Claro The completely undeveloped, lesser-known and less-visited Hoyo Claro is around 17km inland from Punta Cana. This off-the-grid spot, no less beautiful than others, can be challenging to find in terms of signage (and poor Google map directions) and involves a walk of around 30 minutes. A caretaker charges admission of around RD$200 to RD$300 per person (local or foreigner price).

Top Tips

Visit on Sundays when the ecological park opens at 9am: when it's not too hot, the birds are still out and you have the place to yourself. Sit quietly at any of the lagoons to see what animals show up. Look out for the broad-billed tody, the yellow-crowned night heron, Hispaniolan tree frogs and the Hispaniolan slider turtle. Birders can book a bird-watching-focused tour (US$25) that spends time at our observation tower and the 30-minute (US$15) tour of our marine conservation center is a great window onto the foundation's sustainability efforts and challenges.

Jake Kheel, *Vice President, Grupo Puntacana Foundation, @fundaciongrupopuntacana*

Listings

BEST OF THE REST

Singular Spots

Montaña Redonda

Dominicanos instagramos flock to this dramatic mountaintop viewpoint on weekends to take photos swinging in sky-high swing sets and the like. The 360-degree mountain and sea views are jaw-dropping – among the DR's most cinematic.

Basílica de Nuestra Señora de la Altagracia

In the inland city of Higüey, this basilica, with a utilitarian concrete facade topped by an elongated arch reaching high into the sky, is one of the most famous cathedrals in the country.

Altos de Chavón

While a trip to a faux-16th-century Italian-Spanish village created by a Paramount movie-set designer in the 1970s won't give you a window into Dominican culture, it's immensely popular.

Isla Catalinita

This tiny uninhabited island on the eastern edge of Parque Nacional Cotubanamá is a common stop on snorkeling and diving tours.

Punta Cana Faves

Brot Bagel Shop $

Slammed at breakfast, this is where Punta Cana comes for its bagel fix. Bagelwiches come in rarely seen flavors like Hummus Supreme and Montecristo, and they also serve breakfast burritos, salads and wraps.

Castaways Bistro $$

Craving southern US comfort food? Head to this Los Corales spot for jambalaya, Cajun-style gumbo and delicious hush puppies.

Terra Negra $$

'Downtown' Los Corales Mexican joint with a top-flight dessert of *tres leche de cacao*.

Restaurante Playa Blanca $$$

This stylish and atmospheric open-air restaurant is within the Puntacana Resort complex; the beach is spectacular, and the Dominican comfort menu has some surprises.

Jellyfish $$$

A Punta Cana institution on Playa Bávaro, known for its fresh oysters, massive seafood platters and specialties like octopus carpaccio.

Oceanfront Doglegs

Casa de Campo Golf Course

Featuring four Pete Dye–designed golf courses, including 'Dye Fore,' with more than a half-dozen of the 27 holes lining dramatic cliffs in Altos de Chavon.

Corales Puntacana

This Tom Fazio–designed course features six beautiful waterfront holes and hosted a PGA tour event in 2018.

FILIPPO CARLOT/SHUTTERSTOCK

Montaña Redonda

La Cana Golf Club

Part of the Puntacana Resort & Club, this 27-hole course designed by PB Dye (the son of golf architect Pete Dye) has some long and challenging par 4s and stunning ocean views.

Punta Espada Cap Cana Golf Club

This Jack Nicklaus Signature golf course is consistently ranked one of the top courses in the Caribbean and in the world's top 100.

Break Out of Your All-Inclusive

Hispaniola Aquatic Adventures

Highly popular party-boat catamaran tours for up to 25 people. Includes snorkeling at Cabeza de Toro as well as lesser-known beaches and swimming holes, and a seafood lunch.

Runners Adventures

Well-established outfitter offering a range of adventure and cultural tours, including visits to a squirrel-monkey reserve, the longest zip line in the Caribbean, horseback riding and 4WD 'buggie' trips.

Marinarium

Popular with families is a snorkeling trip to the Marinarium, a natural offshore pool near Cabeza de Toro; rays, nurse sharks, tropical fish and patches of coral are all on hand.

RH Tours & Excursions

If you are looking to explore the region, this German-owned tour operator offers day trips to Parque Nacional Los Haitises, boat trips to Isla Saona and tours of Santo Domingo's Zona Colonial.

Location Is Everything

El Caney $

This thatch-roofed restaurant with a more modern annex does a brisk business with folks heading out on excursions from Sabana de la Mar. It serves simple but well-done Dominican breakfasts, basic seafood and meat dishes.

STAN BADZ/GETTY IMAGES

Punta Espada Cap Cana Golf Club

La Entradita $$

You'll find a great, raucous, prototypical Dominican scene at this two-story restaurant-cum-bar overlooking a beach 5km west of La Romana. Come nighttime, the bass is pumping.

Huracan Café $$

Chill beach bar, restaurant and sandy lounge out of street view in Los Corales favored by hip expats, residents and trendier tourists. A perfect place to enjoy a *morir soñando* (tasty combination of orange juice, milk, sugar and crushed ice) and waste away a day at the beach.

Onno's $$

Without question, this open-air bar right on El Cortecito's beach is one of the area's best independent spots to order a cocktail, which you can down to DJs spinning.

Scan to find more things to do in Punta Cana & the Southeast online

PENÍNSULA DE SAMANÁ

CAFE CULTURE | BEACHES | MARINE EXPERIENCES

Experience Península de Samaná online

PENÍNSULA DE SAMANÁ

Trip Builder

Laid-back and cosmopolitan, Samaná offers a European-flavored escape with sophisticated, lively coastal towns and several of the DR's best and most secluded beaches, plus natural attractions including waterfalls, underwater geography and North Atlantic humpback whales.

Swim with the fish on a snorkeling or diving trip to **Piedra Bonita** (p129)

full-day tours

Channel your inner Tarzan and Jane in a lush **jungle tree house** near Playa El Valle (p114)

30min from Samaná

Watch majestic humpbacks breaching and diving in **Bahía de Samaná** (p118)

3hr tours

PREVIOUS SPREAD: AURELIOAPHOTO/SHUTTERSTOCK
FROM LEFT: XAVIERARNAU/GETTY IMAGES, DOMCA9/SHUTTERSTOCK, JUDITH LIENERT/SHUTTERSTOCK

Practicalities

MAURITIUS IMAGES GMB/ALAMY

ARRIVING

Aeropuerto Internacional El Catey (aka Aeropuerto Samaná and Juan Bosch International Airport) Located around 40km west of Samaná, on the highway between Nagua and Sánchez. Receives international flights mainly from Montreal on Air Canada, plus charter flights from the US in high season. Most people fly into Santo Domingo, Punta Cana or Puerto Plata airport, before traveling by car or bus to Samaná.

HOW MUCH FOR A

ATV rental per day US$50

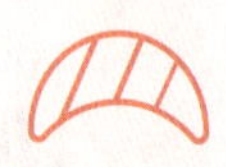

Croissant RD$72

Snorkeling trip US$55

GETTING AROUND

Guagua and bus Local buses, minivans and the like connect the major towns on the peninsula with frequent, affordable services. Comfort isn't always ideal. A few large companies, including Caribe Tours, offer long-distance bus services to Santo Domingo and Puerto Plata.

Taxi A convenient, if relatively pricey way of getting around.

Rental vehicle A car is an excellent way to explore the peninsula on your own or to reach it conveniently from Santo Domingo. Otherwise, motorcycles and ATVs are commonly rented and are great for reaching places closer to your base.

WHEN TO GO

JAN–MAR
North Atlantic humpback whales put on a show in the bay's waters.

APR–JUN
Pleasant weather and thinner crowds, especially earlier in the season.

JUL–SEP
August, in particular, sees loads of Europeans flocking to Las Terrenas.

OCT–DEC
Hurricane season can bring storms; early December offers dry, pleasant days.

TOP: TOMEQS/SHUTTERSTOCK
BOTTOM: CHRIST MO T/SHUTTERSTOCK

EATING & DRINKING

A mélange of culinary influences, where *pains au chocolate* are more common than local *comida criolla* (Creole food). There's always a bounty of fresh seafood, most commonly *mero* (grouper) or *chillo* (red snapper), served in one of four ways: *al ajillo* (with garlic), *al coco* (in coconut sauce), *al criolla* (with a mild tomato sauce) or *a la diabla* (with a spicy tomato sauce). Other seafood, such as *cangrejo* (crab), *calamar* (squid), *camarones* (shrimp), *pulpo* (octopus) and *langosta* (lobster), are similarly prepared or *al vinagre* (in vinegar sauce).

Best gelato
Gelatera Italiana (p131)

Must-try shrimp empanadas
Empanadas y Más (p131)

CONNECT & FIND YOUR WAY

Wi-fi The strength of your signal might depend on how far from town you are, but don't be surprised by spotty connection.

Navigation Roads on major routes are paved and in generally good condition; however, reaching more rural areas and far-flung beaches can threaten compact cars with low axles.

WHERE TO STAY

In Samaná's charming coastal towns, you can have the best of both worlds: access to beautiful beaches plus modern comforts and amenities.

Places	Pros/Cons
Las Terrenas	Wide, high-quality selection; walkable to bars, cafes and restaurants. Traffic congestion and noise.
Beaches near Las Terrenas	Peaceful, varied beachfront identities; boutique to resort options. Need transportation into town; fewer restaurants.
Las Galeras	Unique small boutique options. Beachfront accommodations in short supply.
Playa Valle	More rural, isolated and quiet. Shortage of eating options
Samaná	Closest to whale watching and Los Haitises day-trip departures. Subpar choices.

FROM SANTO DOMINGO

It's less than two hours by car along the extremely well-maintained DR-7 highway from Santo Domingo to Samaná. The toll road costs RD$978 if you continue to Las Terrenas.

MONEY

There are plenty of ATMs in the major towns, but it's not unheard of for some to be short of cash or have low withdrawal limits. It's best to arrive with a fair amount of pesos on hand.

12 Treetop LIVING

VIEWS | NATURE | CULTURE

Channel your inner Tarzan or Jane in lush jungle tree houses near Playa El Valle, 10km north of the coastal town of Samaná. Overnighting in this rural area is a wonderful counterpoint to developed tourism elsewhere, although it's likely coming. For now, disconnect, breathe in the fresh air and live, for a few days at least, entirely alfresco.

How To

Getting around While near the northern coastline, Playa El Valle and Dominican Tree House Village are only accessible by a single road (*guagua*, taxi or rental) coming from the south. Once there, places are walkable, or rent an ATV or motorbike.

Connection Wi-fi, as well as electricity, is less dependable in these parts; there are occasional brownouts associated with periodic strong rains.

Arachnophobia Bugs, mosquitoes and, yes, spiders are unsurprisingly common. Bring and use repellent.

Dominican Tree House Village It's not everyday you can live out your dream of sleeping in a stilted cabin in the jungle, but at one of the country's most unusually situated accommodations, the Dominican Tree House Village, you can. Tucked discreetly away in a dense and lush jungle-clad riverside slope, most of the tree houses are open on three sides and feature queen beds and hammock chairs – all with a dose of privacy and dramatic tropical-forest views. Several larger 'VIP' cabins have outdoor hot-water showers and attached bathrooms.

Right Dominican Tree House Village

DOMCA9/SHUTTERSTOC

Birds, lizards and frogs might become your roommates. Guests mingle over drinks and meals in the bar and lounge – like the tree houses, all constructed from 98% organic material and calling on a twisted climbing-root support system known as *bejuco* to help hold it all together – before heading down for a bit of rum at one of the property firepits. Breakfast and dinner are included.

Get outside A 13-station zip line over the treetops, one of the most thrilling in the Caribbean, horseback riding, as well as a riverine walk to nearby Cascada Lulû, are worth doing.

Other options Several other places have got in on the act, capitalizing on the area's rusticity and mountainous fresh air with lofty lodgings built with local architectural features, including **Zaria Eco Hotel**, **Taino Beach Lofts**, **El Valle Lodge** and **Bungalows India**. Camping on the beach is also allowed (US$20).

Playa El Valle

Need a sunny respite from your arboreal environs? No problem. This is the DR after all. The 4km relatively unspoiled and spectacular **Playa El Valle** is only a short *motoconcho* ride away (arrange with your accommodations). Several restaurants along the beach serve up grilled seafood and dole out the beers. Waters are good for surfing and you can explore a shallow, narrow channel at the far western end, where the Río San Juan empties into the ocean, for a little freshwater cleansing. You can even rent a boat to take you to the remote and beautiful Playa Ermitano.

13 Waterfall PLUNGE

HIKING | SWIMMING | DAY TRIP

Forgo the *ranchos* (horse stalls) lining the roadway through the small town of El Limón and strap on waterproof hiking shoes to make your way by foot through surprisingly rough landscape, surrounded by peaks covered in lush greenery, to 52m Cascada El Limón. Wash off the sweat and mud from your journey with a plunge in the fall's cool, beautiful swimming hole.

VALENTIN VALKOV/SHUTTERSTOCK

How To

When to go Get started early to have some privacy on your swim at the base of the falls. Skip the trip after heavy rains when the path can become nearly impassable.

Getting there *Guaguas* from Las Terrenas (RD$100) leave every half-hour from near the cemetery at the main intersection in town.

Keep an eye out for The DR's national bird, the palmchat, the Hispaniolan woodpecker and the broad-billed tody may all be seen here.

NEIL BOWMAN/SHUTTERSTOCK

MATYAS REHAK/SHUTTERSTOCK

Botom left Palmchat **Top left** Aerial view of Cascada El Limón **Left** Smaller waterfall near Cascada El Limón

Cascada El Limón Despite what some villagers in El Limón will tell you, especially horseback guides, you don't need a guide or a horse to visit the falls. The self-guided walk, around 2.6km each way, can be a slog in parts (and horse manure is everywhere), but the scenery and autonomy are more than enough compensation.

Finding your way It's a minimum 40-minute walk from the main intersection in El Limón, sometimes up a very steep trail over rough terrain with a river or two to ford. It's not difficult to follow the path once you find it: keep your nose open for the scent of freshly roasted cacao. At the top of the first hill, you'll come to a small, old blue-and-yellow house (El Limón is visible in the distance); pass through a narrow opening in a fence on the right, then walk through a nicely manicured grassy area before returning to the oft-muddy path. You will need to pay the entrance fee (RD$50) at a kiosk at the top of the falls. Behind the souvenir shop near the entrance kiosk are vertiginous views looking down the falls. It's a short, steep hike down to the falls from here.

Packing notes Wear sturdy water shoes and bring a towel: a smaller falls with a pool ideal for swimming is accessible on the return hike.

By Horseback

There are almost a dozen *paradas* (horseback-riding operations) in town and on the highway toward Samaná offering tours. Prices range from US$65 to US$100 for the 30- to 60-minute ride up the hill to the waterfalls, 30 to 60 minutes at the falls to take a dip and enjoy the scene, and a 30- to 60-minute return trip, with lunch at the end. Your guide – who you should tip 15% to 20% – will be walking, not riding, as is the custom.

Whether you walk or go on horseback, you will get wet as there are several river crossings along the way – rubber sandals are a good idea.

14 WHALE of a Time

BOAT CRUISE | WILDLIFE WATCHING | DAY TRIP

Every year, thousands of humpback whales congregate in the waters off the Península de Samaná to mate and give birth, watched by boatloads of their human fans, often North Americans and Europeans who have also migrated south to the Caribbean. Get a front-row seat to this spectacle, including mothers and their babies trying out their fins for the first time.

JENYA_TARASOF/SHUTTERSTOCK

How To

Getting there *Guaguas* connect Samaná to Las Galeras (one hour, every 15 minutes) and Las Terrenas (1¼ hours, every 90 minutes).

When to go Mid-January to mid-March are good times to visit, with February being peak season for humpbacks. Make reservations as far in advance as possible during major holidays.

Lunch on the *malecón* Pre- or post-whale watching, stroll along Samaná's waterfront avenue for a lunch of grilled seafood and the like.

JENYA_TARASOF/SHUTTERSTOCK

ADISHA PRAMOD/ALAMY

Bottom left Humpback whale, Bahía de Samaná **Top left** Humpback whale breaching **Left** Mother and calf humpback whales

Bahía de Samaná For sheer awe-inspiring natural-world sublimity, a whale-watching trip is hard to beat and the Bahía de Samaná is considered to be one of the top destinations in the world. The cat's long been out of the bag: around 60,000 people travel here yearly for the show. You are all but guaranteed to see numerous humpback whales surfacing for air, lifting their fins or tail, jostling each other in competition, and even breaching – impressive jumps followed by an equally impressive splash. You'll no doubt spot loads of dolphins skimming the surface as well. It can be a rough trip for those prone to seasickness; come prepared with motion-sickness medication and aids, and plenty of sunscreen.

Responsible whale-watching A manual of responsible behavior was created for operators and every year all stakeholders renew their commitment. Minimum boat sizes are regulated: in big seas small boats are low to the water and sometimes aren't aware of the whales until they are too close. Private vessels of any size are prohibited near the whales and are only allowed transit into or out of the bay. Do your part by not utilizing illegal operators.

Heading out Most of the whale-watching companies depart from Samaná and run a morning and afternoon trip. Each trip lasts three to four hours, depending on sightings. There's little difference in terms of your likelihood of seeing whales, and although the water may be slightly rougher in the afternoon, it also tends to be quieter, with fewer boats out. There are over 40 vessels with legal permits.

Under Threat

Threats to the humpback whale population of Samaná are increasing. Two major cruise ship ports – one, a tender port in front of the pedestrian bridge right in the town of Samaná and the other 14km west in Arroyo Barril – were approved by the Dominican government. This development promises more than 250 cruise ships and over half a million passengers during the whale-watching season in the near future. In recent years, there were 30 ships on average. There's significant concern that due to this dramatically increased traffic, and the associated stress on the whales' environment, they will be displaced from one of their most important reproductive areas in the North Atlantic.

Kim Bedall, *owner Whale Samana, facebook.com/whalesamana*

Behold Leviathan

GET THE LOWDOWN ON WHALES WHO MIGRATE TO SAMANÁ

Bahía de Samaná is one of the world's largest singles bars – for whales. From mid-January to mid-March, humpbacks come here to mate and calve, with an average of 12 new calves born each year.

BERNARD RADVANER/GETTY IMAGES

Why Here?

Humpback whales migrate to Bahía de Samaná each year, attracted by the bay's specific profile, including depths of around 20m to 25m, which means good sound transmission. The wind conditions and temperature are just right for calves, who lack layers of blubber to insulate them from cold, as is the salinity of the bay mouth; marine scientists speculate that one of the reasons they enter the less saline waters inside the bay is to cleanse themselves of parasites – adult humpbacks carry on average 1 tonne.

Repeat Visitors

Experienced watchers are able to identify regular visitors years after a previous spotting by their distinctive fluke markings. DR-based scientists and amateur cetologists exchange info with colleagues all along the whales' northern return path, an up to nine-week journey of 3000km to 7000km to the far North Atlantic where they feed. There's a catalog identifying over 10,000 individual whales, some with distinctive names such as Aramis or Dog Ear.

Good to Know

If humpbacks had a motto, it might be 'go big or go home': everything about them is supersized! Their average lifespan typically ranges from 80 to 90 years. The length of healthy adults is a whopping 13m to 16m. They eat up to 1½ tonnes of krill, plankton and small fish a day. And they can stay submerged for up to 30 minutes, though dives more typically last 15 minutes. Also, whale urine is immensely beneficial to the marine ecosystem; phytoplankton feeds on it.

Left Mother and calf humpback whales **Center** A whale surfaces near a whale-watching boat **Right** Divers explore an underwater shipwreck

KIT KORZUN/GETTY IMAGES

MATTIE LEYDEN/GETTY IMAGES

Threats

With no history of whaling, the DR has worked to promote responsible whale-watching in the wider Caribbean and joined the International Whaling Commission in 2009. Japan, Norway and Iceland are the only countries that continue commercial whaling; Norway and Iceland catch North Atlantic common minke whales with 'official reservations' or 'objections' to the moratorium, while Japan is 'unbound'. Some indigenous communities in Alaska, Russia, Greenland, and St Vincent and the Grenadines practice subsistence whaling for cultural and nutritional purposes.

> If humpbacks had a motto, it might be 'go big or go home': everything about them is supersized!

Humpbacks are a coastal species, which means they brush up against humans and everything that comes with us (climate change, pollution, overdevelopment, boating and fishing). Yet, they are remarkably tolerant and resilient. Once listed as a 'vulnerable' species on the International Union for Conservation of Nature's Red List, in 2018 they were recategorized globally as 'of less concern.' Still, because they occupy shallow waters close to shore where there's intense human activity, including large cruise ships, as well as unlicensed and irresponsible whale-watching, the impact of our commingling in the Caribbean isn't fully understood.

Underwater Cemetery

Humpbacks share the Bahía de Samaná with a veritable graveyard of ships, some ripped apart by hurricanes, others plundered by pirates. Two famous galleons, the *Nuestra Señora de Guadalupe* and *El Conde de Tolasa*, sank on August 25, 1724, within hours of one another. They remained undiscovered for more than 250 years until 1976 and 1977, respectively. Both ships were en route to Mexico when a violent storm forced them from the shore toward a treacherous reef where they were torn apart and sank, with over 600 passengers on board. Among the thousands of items discovered at the wreck sites were hundreds of gold coins minted in Spain in the early 18th century.

15 Peninsula Beach DELIGHTS

SUN | WATER SPORTS | DINING

For those who are connoisseurs of such things, Samaná's more than two dozen beaches, ranging from cliff-backed secluded coves to action-packed, lively ones akin to a sandy town plaza, merit accolades. Try out your fair share, but you might want your favorites to yourself.

GUYMCQUEEN/SHUTTERSTOCK

How To

Getting around Get a boat, *motoconcho* or walk to beaches around Las Galeras; in Las Terrenas, rent a motorbike or ATV to fit in with locals.

What to do on the water Paddleboarding, kayaking, surfing, windsurfing, kitesurfing, hyrdrofoiling, wakeboarding, snorkeling, scuba diving, horseback riding and catamaran trips are all options.

Lunch on the beach A whole lobster, fried octopus, rice and *tostones* (fried plantains) for two runs around RD$1500; throw in a *coco frío* (chilled coconut water) for a few more pesos.

WWW.GGGPHOTO.COM/SHUTTERSTOCK

Las Galeras

Around the small one-main-intersection fishing community of **Las Galeras** at the far eastern tip of Samaná, everything ends at a beach: the roads, the days, your daily ambitions. The first stop on a day-long 'safari' is usually **Playa Fronton**, dramatically backed by dark, volcanic cliffs. Beware of sea urchins on your way out from the beach to do some snorkeling. You can walk here from town. **Playa Madama** is another small stretch, backed by palm trees with a few caves to explore; unfortunately, littering is a bit of an issue and sunlight is in short supply in the afternoon. Wild and stunning **Playa Colorado**, which is only visited by boats, works as a lunch stop.

Playa Rincón is the well-established highlight. No longer a have-it-to-yourself destination, you can nevertheless find your own spot

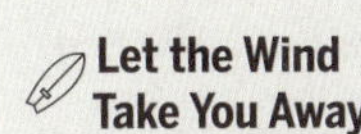

Let the Wind Take You Away

The beaches around Las Terrenas, especially Punta Popy, are great for taking up, practicing or simply watching kiteboarding. A number of kitesurfing schools are nearby and all offer multiday certification courses in this adrenaline-pumping sport.

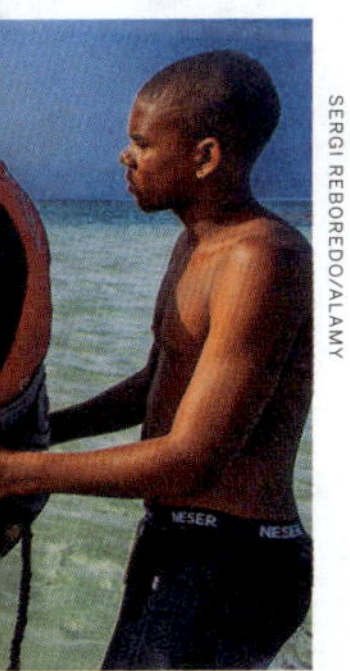
SERGI REBOREDO/ALAMY

Left Kitesurfing lessons, Las Terrenas (p125) **Top left** Playa Fronton **Above** Aerial view of Playa Rincón

for privacy somewhere along its palm tree–lined 3km stretch. At the far western end, where the Río Caño Frio flows into the ocean, dip into the three jade-colored mangrove pools, identified by locals as Love, Children and Divorce. The last has the clearest water, but beware: it's said that its eponymous fate will befall whoever jumps in.

Companies like **Samana Tourist Services** charge US$65/35 per person with/without food for day-long trips that hit all of the above. Waters can be rough, so this one's best avoided by those prone to seasickness (or take some motion-sickness medication) and those interested in more privacy; boats usually carry a dozen others.

Playita, far better than the town beach, and only a short walk or *motoconcho* ride away, is a swath of tannish sand with mellow surf, backed by palm trees and a few thatched-roof informal restaurants. It's a great option for those looking to stick close to town.

Whale-Spotting

The best beach close to the town of Samaná, in the Bahía de Samaná, is **Cayo Levantado** (aka 'Bacardi Island'). The eastern side is occupied by a luxury resort; however, there's a nearly unreal-looking public beach on the western half, with unspoiled sugar-white sands fringed by swaying palms and impossibly turquoise waters. Visitors can kayak, paddleboard, swim or enjoy a lunch of freshly caught fish. Those who are very lucky might spot a whale breaching from the shore.

Boat taxi at Samaná port can get you there, or purchase a Cayo Levantado day pass through a tour operator.

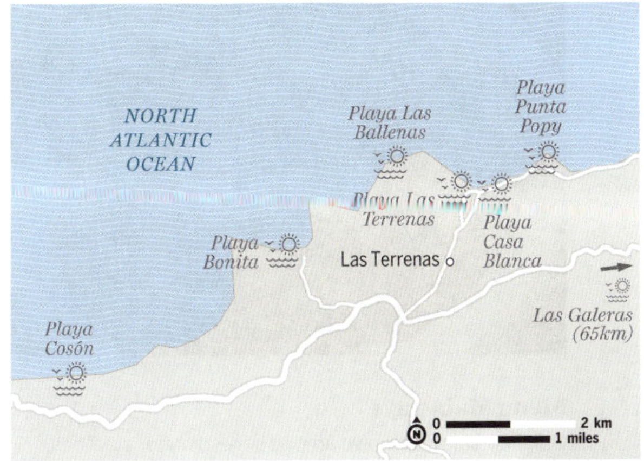

Las Terrenas

Las Terrenas has an equally robust choice of beaches, with perhaps even a larger amount of accessible ones than Las Galeras since all can be reached by roads. **Playa Las Terrenas** and **Playa Casa Blanca** flank the center of town, bookended by the calmer sands of **Playa Las Ballenas** (to the west) and wind-whipped **Playa Punta Popy** (to the east); the waters of the latter are filled with kitesurfers and windsurfers. Theoretically, you can walk all the way from the steep and narrow, but beautiful, half-moon-shaped **Playa Bonita**, where several quality boutique hotels make this a great spot to base yourself, to the sands of Cosón Bay and on to the long, seemingly never-ending stretch of **Playa Cosón** – but bring plenty of water.

There's no shortage of other stunning, less-visited beaches further east and west. Most are best accessed by your own rental vehicle or on a day-long boat or catamaran trip.

Left Cayo Levantado **Below** Playita

FROM LEFT: ONAPALMTREE/SHUTTERSTOCK, JON ARNOLD IMAGES LTD/ALAMY

More than Rice & Beans

TAKE YOUR TASTE BUDS ON A DOMINICAN TOUR

Ditch the resort buffet and try Dominican cuisine *(comida criolla),* a hybrid of Spanish, African and indigenous flavors and styles. There's so much more on offer than the *'plato del dia'* (set menu), and the act of eating and drinking in the DR is the social glue that binds people together.

Left *Locrio* with salami **Center** Tropical fruit stall, Samaná **Right** Typical Dominican breakfast

IMAGE PROFESSIONALS GMBH/ALAMY

Menu Mainstays

Culinary staples revolve around several major starches, including rice, potatoes, bananas, yucca and cassava, usually served in large portions – leave your low-carb diet at home. Filling, cheap and nearly ubiquitous is *la bandera* (the flag), a Dominican dish of white rice, *habichuela* (red beans), stewed meat, salad and fried green plantains. Another hearty specialty, *mofongo,* involves mashed plantains mixed most often with pork rinds. *Locrio,* a Dominican version of paella made with achiote-colored rice, *habichuela con dulce,* a root vegetable–based soup, and *chivo* (goat), done in a number of ways, are often found on menus.

Street Food

One of the great pleasures of eating in the DR is sampling specialties served from beachside or streetside vendors. Grab a few *pastelitos,* similar to empanadas (another satisfying on-the-go meal). The former are usually filled with beef or chicken, which has been stewed with onions, olives, tomatoes and a variety of seasonings, then chopped up and mixed with peas, nuts and raisins, before being tucked into a patty of dough and fried in boiling oil. *Chimi* are sandwiches of seasoned ground meat, cooked cabbage, carrots, red onions and tomatoes, typically served in a plastic bag to catch the juices. *Yaniqueques* (or Johnny cakes), a greasy fried cornmeal flatbread popular with beach hawkers, can be washed down with fresh coconut water or a *frío-frío,* the Dominican version of a snow cone. Originating in Santiago, *yaraos,* similar to Canadian poutine, is a gut-busting mash of French fries, cheese and grilled beef topped with ketchup and mayo. And don't

ROBERTO BINETTI/SHUTTERSTOCK

STARLING JIMENEZ/SHUTTERSTOCK

miss out on a fried trio of *frituras de batata* (sweet-potato fritters), *fritos maduros* (ripe plantain fritters) and the ubiquitous *tostones* (fried plantain slices).

Tropical Fruit

Besides being refreshing and nutritious, among the most aesthetically pleasing sights are the tropical fruits arranged in towering piles along roadway kiosks. The list of bounty is long, but the following are worth noting and are served cut up, ready to eat or juiced: mango, guavaberry, papaya, dragon fruit, starfruit, pineapple, guava, guanabana, sapodilla and ambarella.

> One of the great pleasures of eating in the DR is sampling specialties served from beachside or streetside vendors.

Meals

For *campesinos* (rural Dominicans), breakfast is usually a heavy meal, but for other Dominicans, lunch and dinner compete for most important meal of the day. All three usually consist of one main dish – eggs for breakfast and meat for lunch and dinner – served with one or more accompaniments, usually fresh fruit, rice, beans, salad and/or boiled vegetables. Hole-in-the-wall eateries called *comedores* are generally good spots to try out the basics. Fried chicken lovers will be well served by thick-on-the-ground *pica pollo* places, their single-minded specialty, but restaurants in cities and popular tourist areas cater to international tastes and culinary fare.

Just Say No

The seasonal ban from July through October on the harvesting and serving of what Dominicans (and Haitians) call *lambi* (conch, pronounced 'konk'), means you can do your part by not ordering it if you see it on a menu. It's a fairly ubiquitous dish and this hefty snail-like creature, often served in salads, soups and curries, is no doubt tasty. But it's also a vital part of the underwater ecosystem and a valuable fishery resource. Stocks have shrunk considerably in the Caribbean and the seasonal ban allows them to reproduce in order to maintain healthy population levels.

16 Under the SEA

SCUBA DIVING | SNORKELING | MARINE LIFE

The cooler waters of the Península de Samaná's Atlantic-facing coastline means more varied underwater terrain and, while rare, divers have reported hearing humpback whales singing. Even if you have hundreds of dives logged, how can you pass up that opportunity? Throw in a couple of charming towns and you'll soon see the appeal of centering a Samaná trip around the sea.

INGOLF POMPE 7/ALAMY

How To

When to go There are fewer storms and calmer seas from May to September; bad weather might cancel trips for days at a time from October to April.

Plan ahead Most dive shops also run snorkeling trips, sometimes simultaneously. There are plenty of operators in Las Terrenas and Las Galeras, but it's best to ask around (and check online reviews) before settling on one.

Costs Day-long snorkeling boat trips are around US$65 per person, whereas two boat dives with equipment included is US$95.

INGOLF POMPE 7/ALAMY

MAURITIUS IMAGES GMBH/ALAMY

Bottom left Divers surface, Las Galeras **Top left** Redspotted hawkfish **Left** Cabo Cabrón

Las Terrenas There are plenty of relatively shallow sites with some healthy coral only about 10 to 15 minutes from Las Terrenas by boat. One favorite of ours is a **wreck** in 28m of water and **Isla Las Ballenas**, visible from shore, with a large underwater cave. Most operators also offer special trips to **Dudu Cave**, a sinkhole with natural spring water–fed caverns near Río San Juan. One popular full-day snorkeling trip is to **Playa Jackson**, several kilometers west of town and reached by boat.

Las Galeras Several popular dive sites around Las Galeras worth highlighting are **Piedra Bonita**, a 50m stone tower good for spotting jacks, barracudas and sea turtles; **Cathedral**, an enormous underwater cave opening to sunlight; and a sunken 55m container ship haunted by big morays. Several large, shallow coral patches, including **Los Carriles**, a series of underwater hills, are good for beginner divers.

For experienced divers, **Cabo Cabrón** (Bastard Point) is one of the north coast's best. After an easy boat ride from Las Galeras, you're dropped into a churning channel with a giant coral formation that you can swim around; dolphins frequent the area.

Or book a snorkeling-only trip out to the reefs, some of the best on the peninsula, around **Playa Frontón**.

Jackson Bay

Jackson Bay, just off Playa Jackson to the west of Las Terrenas, is one of the best snorkeling sites in the DR. The fairly shallow reefs (means they get plenty of light) are pristine and you'll see parrotfish, blue cromis, trumpet fish, sergeant fish, damsel fish, and sometimes an eagle ray, a remora or turtle. Relatively secluded, there are no hotels or development, so no polluting run-off from streams. Fishers tend to be in very small boats, even rowing. Because the bay is partially sheltered from storms, at one time it was a natural mooring for ships around 400 years ago.

Recommended by *Paul Williamson, owner of Las Terrenas Dive Academy, @tda_lasterrenas*

Listings

BEST OF THE REST

Food with Views

El Cabito $$$

The road here from Las Galeras is rough, but the journey is worth it. Enjoy heaping plates of fresh seafood while perched on a commanding cliff with hawks overhead and whales in the distance.

El Monte Azul $$

Clinging spectacularly to the edge of a cliff outside Las Galeras, El Monte Azul offers postcard-perfect views and a good-value menu split between French-leaning meat and seafood, and a variety of noodle dishes.

El Lugar $$

Fulfills carnivorous desires with juicy, rich burgers and wood-fired steaks, plus lobster and fish, all served within a trendy ambience. Views of the Las Terrenas stylish set and sunsets are enjoyed from the 2nd floor.

Bárrio Latíno Cafe $$

The views here are of people. Occupying the busiest corner in Las Terrenas, this open-sided brasserie has an eclectic international menu.

Dining with Sand in Your Toes

Raquel's Sunset Bar $

This beachfront shack at the end of the road in Las Galeras is ideal for a fresh coconut, pineapple or cocktail.

La Terrasse $$

The best of the bunch on Las Terrenas' gourmet promenade along the beach, with a sophisticated French bistro menu deserving a Michelin star or two.

Paco Cabana $$

French cuisine meets Caribbean in this alfresco Las Terrenas beachfront spot with cushy couches, candlelit tables and chilled cocktails.

Restaurante Luís $$

Dig your toes into Playa Cosón's sand, shoot the breeze with the server (there's no menu), and wait for tasty lobsters and fresh fish.

Underwater Terrain

Las Galeras Divers

Well-respected, French-run dive shop at Las Galeras' main intersection. One-/two-tank dives including all equipment cost US$55/85; US$10 less if you have your own gear.

Diving Scuba Libre

Located along the road to La Playita in Las Galeras, in addition to diving, it offers snorkeling trips plus windsurfer and catamaran rental and instruction.

Dive Academy

This Las Terrenas English-run NAUI outfitter also offers snorkeling and charter trips.

Playa las Flechas

Lovely Landmarks

Playa las Flechas

This small beach, 5km east of Samaná, is thought by many historians to be the site of a short battle between Columbus' crew and the Ciguayos, a Taíno *cacique* (chiefdom)

Boca del Diablo (Mouth of the Devil)

Waves rush up a natural channel and blast out of this impressive blowhole in the rocks southeast of Las Galeras. Getting here involves taking a car or motorcycle over a rough road.

Let Them Lead the Way

Whale Samaná

Samaná's most respected and longest-running whale-watching outfit, owned and operated by Canadian marine-mammal specialist Kim Beddall. The company uses a large two-deck boat with capacity for 60 people.

Tour Samaná with Terry

Day trips to El Limón, whale-watching (working alongside Whale Samaná), and more adventurous horseback-riding/zip-lining and quad-biking/zip-lining combos.

LT'Kite

Recommended kitesurfing school run by a friendly Frenchman. It rents surfboards and kitesurfing equipment, and provides lessons and IKO certifications for the latter.

Flora Tours

French-run agency known for ecosensitive tours to Parque Nacional Los Haitises, hard-to-access beaches, as well as tranquil catamaran trips, and culturally sensitive quad-bike tours to remote villages.

ZOONAR GMBH/ALAMY

Boca del Diablo (Mouth of the Devil)

Come-as-You-Are Restaurants

Empanadas y Más $

This hole-in-the-wall Las Terrenas spot raises empanadas into an art form. Try the ceviche and *guanabana* (soursop) juice.

Boulangerie Française $

The street-side patio practically feels like Montmartre, and it serves the best croissants, pastries and espresso in Las Terrenas.

Gelatera Italiana $

Continental-quality gelato is served up at this small spot in Las Terrenas.

Restaurant Lila $

On the main road in Las Galeras, this casual open-air place serves basic but filling Dominican standards.

Royal Snack $

Across from the ferry dock in Samaná, this simple French-run cafe is a good bet for French-leaning quick meals, burgers and salads throughout the day.

Presidente
Experience North Coast online

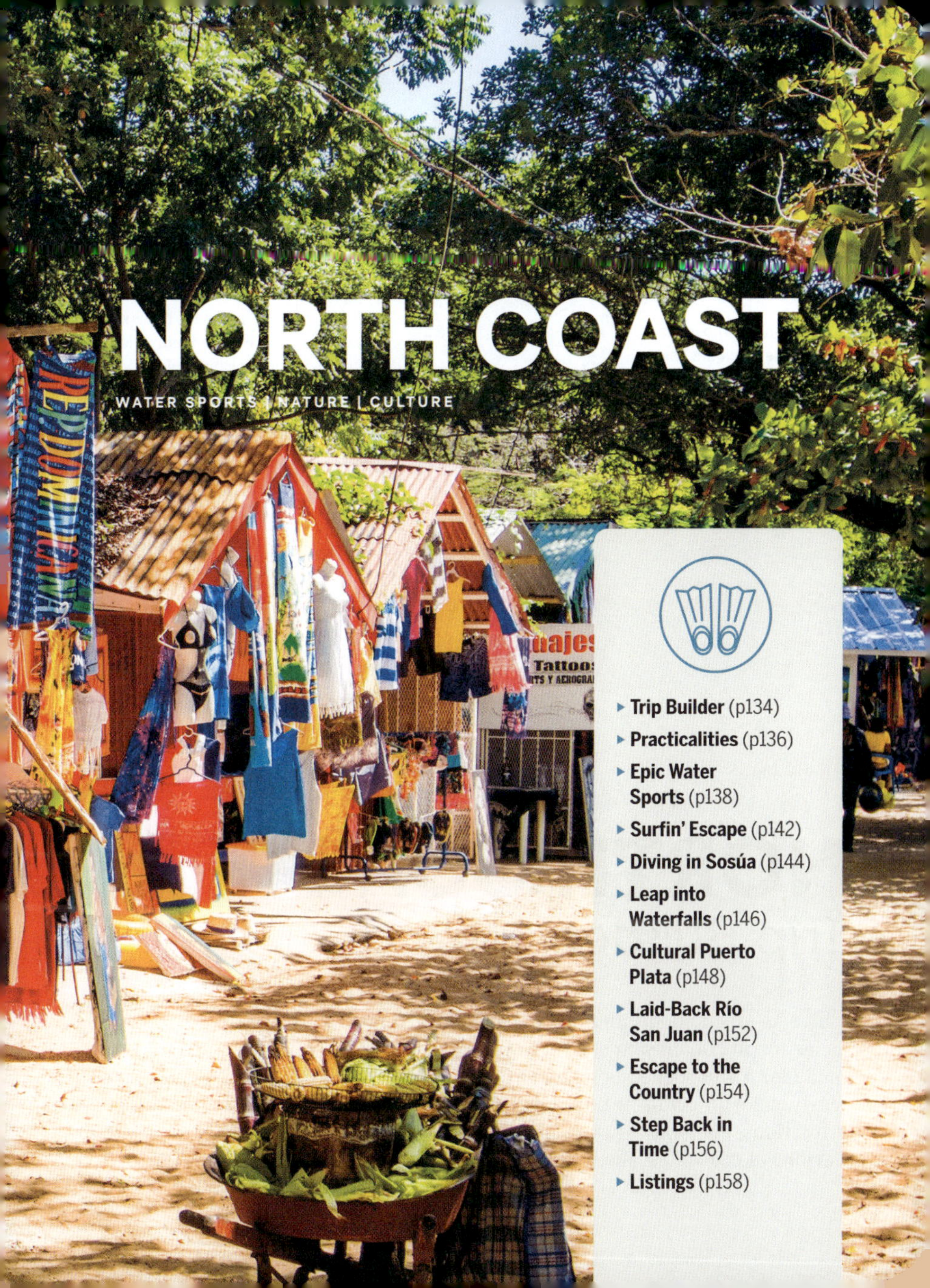

NORTH COAST

WATER SPORTS | NATURE | CULTURE

NORTH COAST
Trip Builder

As much about landing gnarly kiteboard moves as lazing on golden sands, DR's North Coast is tailor-made for a sun-soaked holiday. Throw in seafood feasts, colorful corals, tranquil waterfalls and cultural attractions, and you've got yourself the perfect Caribbean coastal escape.

0 50 km
0 25 miles

Strap on the mask to explore corals around **Sosúa** (p144)
15min from Puerto Plata Airport

Catch a wave at **Playa Encuentro**, DR's most consistent surf break (p143)
10min from Cabarete

Kitesurf with the pros at **Cabarete** (p138)
30min from Puerto Plata Airport

Enjoy long walks on the beach at **Playa Grande** (p153)
1½hr from Puerto Plata Airport

Sosúa
Cabarete
Sabaneta de Yasica
5
Jamao Al Norte
Río San Juan
Abreu
Magante
José Contreras
Río Boba
Moca
Tenares
Nagua
San Francisco de Macorís
Villa Tapia
La Vega

Practicalities

MATYAS REHAK/SHUTTERSTOCK

ARRIVING

Aeropuerto Internacional Las Américas If arriving from Santo Domingo's main international airport, you'll slice through the country from south to north in a 246km bus journey to Puerto Plata in four hours.

Aeropuerto Internacional Gregorio Luperón Known as Puerto Plata Airport (pictured), this is the most convenient arrival point; 18km west of Puerto Plata, 8km east of Sosúa and 20km from Cabarete.

HOW MUCH FOR A

Bottled beer RD$150–300

Seafood meal RD$500–1000

Kiteboarding from US$80

WHEN TO GO

DEC–MAR
Winds pick up, making it ideal for surfing. Peak season dry months bring the best weather.

MAY–AUG
Peak kitesurfing winds during these months

JUN
Cabarete's Jazz Festival is in full swing

SEP
Check out the best exponents in the Master of the Ocean competition.

GETTING AROUND

Guagua The most inexpensive and practical means of traveling between towns are *guaguas* (local buses), which come and go along the coastal highway. They pass by nearly every 30 minutes from 6am to 5pm.

Car/taxi/Uber Hiring a car makes a lot of sense if you plan on tackling the entire coastline. Otherwise, taxis or less-costly Ubers are good for short jaunts around towns.

Motoconcho Cheaper and easier to find than taxis, *motoconchos* (motorcycle taxis) are the best, and sometimes only, way to get around in many towns. Request a helmet if you can.

EATING & DRINKING

Fresh seafood is a highlight of the North Coast. From casual beachside shacks to crisp white-linen restaurants, this is the place to indulge in freshly caught grilled fish, lobster, calamari and shrimp. Thanks to expats from France, Italy and the US, the region also has some standout international cuisine. But don't miss out on local Dominican specialties (that's why you're here!), including grilled herb-fed goat meat. For drinks, Cabarete, Sosúa and Puerto Plata are your go-to spots for beachfront beers, mojitos and piña coladas.

Best sunset drinks
Velero Sunset Grill (p159)

Must try empanadas
La Casona (p161)

TOP: OLEKSANDRA IABLOCHNIKOVA/GETTY IMAGES
BOTTOM: WANDERLUST MEDIA/SHUTTERSTOCK

CONNECT & FIND YOUR WAY

Wi-fi Generally fast given the North Coast is favored by foreign expats and tourists; free wi-fi is offered widely across accommodations and many restaurants.

Navigation There shouldn't be any issues finding your way around these coastal towns. If not on foot, Uber or *motoconchos* will zip from door to door.

WHERE TO STAY

Your specific interests – whether it's beaches, surfing, diving or local culture – will largely influence which town you choose to stay in.

Towns	Pros/Cons
Cabarete	Ground zero for kiteboarders, surfers and backpackers seeking a vibrant, happening nightlife that kicks on late.
Sosúa	The pick for beaches and nightlife. Still struggling to shed its seedy reputation.
Puerto Plata	Atmospheric old town offering boutique stays in heritage mansions.
Río San Juan	Very good option for those seeking resorts, villas and luxury hotels close to the beach.

FIND YOUR BEACH

With a long coastline of beautiful beaches, discovering your perfect one may require some exploration. Rent a car to find your ideal patch of sand.

MONEY

ATMs are prevalent in the main towns across this coast. Avoid changing money at the airport. US dollars are widely accepted, but have some pesos on hand for smaller businesses.

EPIC
Water Sports

KITEBOARDING | PADDLING | LESSONS

Thrill-seeking riders from around the globe make a beeline for Cabarete, the kiteboarding capital of the Caribbean. But whatever floats your boat (literally) – windsurfing, paddleboarding, wakeboarding, foiling, sailboating – the wind-whipped Atlantic Ocean offers year-round action.

ANDREY PROKHOROV/500P

How To

Getting here & around Cabarete is 18km west of Puerto Plata's airport, from where you can rent a car or take a taxi. Main buses go as far as Sosúa, but plenty of *guaguas* ply the coastal road.

When to go Year-round but peak kiteboarding months are June to August.

Events At the annual celebration of surfing, windsurfing, SUP and kitesurfing, you can watch spectacular **Master of the Ocean** (masteroftheocean.org) performances from the beach.

LAGENTE.DO/SHUTTERSTOCK

Kiteboarding Heaven

Kiteboarders are a fanatical lot who travel far and wide wherever the trade winds blow, so when they hear about a place called **Kite Beach**, naturally eyes are going to light up. One of the undisputed world capitals for kiteboarding, the one-time sleepy fishing hamlet of **Cabarete** is now a happening enclave for the Red Bull swillin' set, here to tear it up with tricks and aerial maneuvers.

Thanks to its strong, steady thermal winds (check windguru.cz), shallow, calm waters and a rock-free shore, both pros and beginners flock here to catch the ride of a lifetime. On its day, Kite Beach is a sight to behold: a sea of color in what is a festival of kites as hundreds of riders descend upon these waters.

CHRISTOPHER V JONES/SHUTTERSTOCK

A Perfect Day

A perfect day kiteboarding in Cabarete starts with a *cafecito*. Midday brings those sweet thermal *brisas* and perfect swells – smashing *olas* on the reef. The day wraps with happy hour mojitos on our beachfront deck, *bachata* playing, *corazón* full.

Jose Luis *Pro kitesurfer, owner of Cabarate Kite Point; @cabaretekitepoint @eloctazocafe*

Left Wingfoiling, Cabarete **Top left** Kitesurfing, Cabarete **Above** Kitesurfer

Cabarete's beaches are lined with world-class operators offering lessons for beginners, intermediates and advanced riders. If Kite Beach feels too crowded or intimidating, **Playa Cabarete** or **Bozo Beach** provide a more relaxed atmosphere, ideal for beginners.

For a quieter, low-key experience, make the journey 170km west to **Buen Hombre** – still an under-the-radar hot spot despite being well-renowned as a kitesurfing destination for over 12 years – run by Miky, a Dominican champion of strapless kitesurfing. And if you're into kitesurfing (basically kiteboarding on a surfboard to ride waves), nearby **Playa Encuentro** is the place to catch Cabarete's beach breaks (p142).

More Water Sports Action

Kiteboarding and surfing aren't the only thrilling ways to enjoy the warm, clear Atlantic waters of DR's North Coast. Add wingfoiling, hydrofoiling, skimboarding and wakeboarding

Kiteboarding Operators

Cabarete Kite Point

Kitesurfing and wingfoiling lessons, equipment rentals and a beachfront cafe (p158) at Kite Beach. (cabaretekitepoint.com)

Laurel Eastman Kiteboarding

Run by one of the world's top kiteboarders, this is a friendly, safety-conscious operation teaching kite- and wingboarding. (laureleastman.com)

Champion Kite School

Popular school on Kite Beach established by a former pro who'll have you kiteboarding before you leave. (championkiteschoolcabarete.com)

Pro Kite Cabarete

Kiteboarding, wingboarding and foil-boarding lessons, one-on-one or in groups. (prokitecabarete.com)

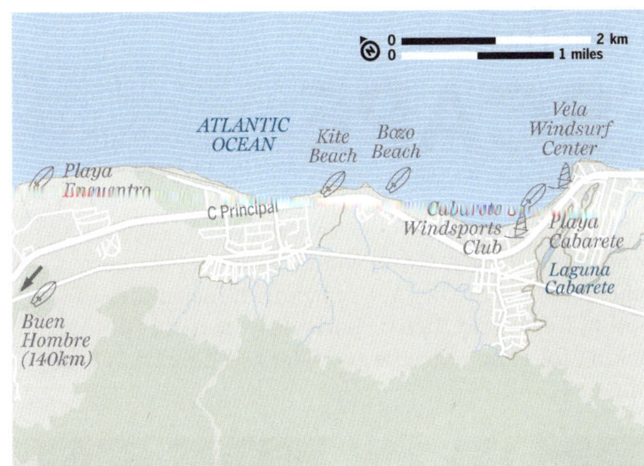

Left Kitesurfer, Cabarete Beach
Below Windsurfing lesson, Cabarete Beach

to your adrenaline-fueled list; all are safer than kiteboarding, available year-round, in any conditions and less dependent on seasonal winds.

By the time you read this, there's likely to be even more new water sports on offer, so ask around. In the meantime, wingfoiling involves a light, hand-held inflatable sail (not attached to the board) while you stand on a board with a submerged hydrofoil that lifts you above the water. Hydrofoiling is similar, but without the hand-held sail – just the hydrofoil board to glide you along.

Otherwise, keep it old-school with windsurfing, the very activity that first put Cabarete on the map back in the 1980s. Not as popular as in days gone by, **Playa Cabarete** is still one of the best spots in the world for it. Book through **Cabarete Windsports Club** (cabaretewindsportsclub.com) or **Vela Windsurf Center** (velawatersports.com/cabarete). The latter also rents out sea kayaks and SUPs if paddling is more your thing. Alternatively, head inland for a leisurely day with **Kayak River Adventures** (kayakriveradventures.com) paddling along the crystal-clear waters of Río Yasica.

Carib Wind (caribwind.com) offers yet another way to enjoy the ocean, renting out Lasers (single-person sailing dinghies) and catamarans, as well as providing lessons.

18 Surfin' ESCAPE

WAVES | LESSONS | PLAYA ENCUENTRO

While Cabarete may be better known for its wind than its waves, here you'll find some of the Caribbean's best breaks. Yet somehow it flies under the radar, with many surfers opting for Puerto Rico or Barbados – leaving DR's North Coast ripe for the picking for experienced wave-riders seeking barrels or those here for their first ride.

MARY BARATTO/GETTY IMAGES

How To

Getting here and around Cabarete is where most surfers base themselves to access nearby breaks, namely Playa Encuentro, 4km west of town. Given the early starts, having your own wheels is handy.

When to go Year-round, but winter months (November to February) produce the best waves.

Early bird catches the wave Get ready for sunrise surfs, as once those winds pick up at around 10am, you can say goodbye to waves for the rest of the day.

GEORGE HARPER/GETTY IMAGES

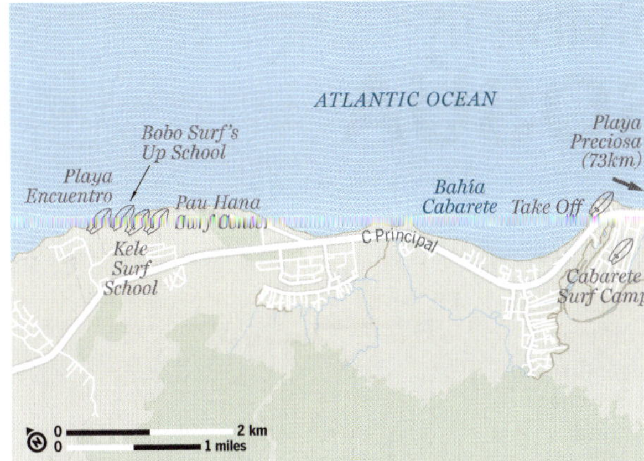

Bottom left Surfer, Cabarete Beach
Top left Surf schools, Playa Encuentro

Playa Encuentro When people talk of surf in Cabarete what they actually mean is Playa Encuentro, 4km west of town. The capital of DR's surf scene, this long stretch of beach with crystal-clear warm waters (leave the wet suit at home) has a selection of five world-class breaks. The most famous is **Coco Pipe**, a hollow, glassy reef break at Encuentro's far east (though watch out for spiny sea urchins in the shallows here). Most consistent is **Encuentro Main Break**, comprising twin breaks **La Derecha** and **Bobo's Point**; the latter is a good wave for learners. At the far western end is the aptly named **Destroyers**, a very shallow and challenging, fast peeling left break that's claimed many a banged-up victim on its reef.

Playa Preciosa Some 60km east of Encuentro you'll find some of DR's biggest and best waves at scenic Playa Preciosa (p153), attracting sunrise surfers for its pounding waves. Though waves can be massive – sometimes as big as 4m monsters – it's worth bringing a small wave board for when conditions aren't working. And though early rises can be a bummer, not only do you get to surf while basking in the ethereal glow of sunrise, but once those winds arrive, kiters get the best of both worlds, having the rest of the day to enjoy all the wind water sports.

Rentals and lessons Surfboard rental for a day is around US$20; a two-hour course costs US$45 to US$50 per person, and a five-day surf camp costs US$200 per person.

Where to Learn

Bobo Surf's Up School
Popular school that's been teaching folk to shred since the 1990s. Accommodations and surf packages too. (bobosurfsup.com)

Cabarete Surf Camp
Lessons, board rental and fantastic accommodations and instructors. Based in Cabarete, it also offers kitesurfing. (cabaretesurfcamp.com)

Kele Surf School
Lessons for all levels with quality boards, instructors and competitive prices. (kelesurf.com)

Pau Hana Surf Camp
One of the first schools on Playa Encuentro, Pau Hana has a good reputation for employing locals and environmental sustainability initiatives. (pauhanasurfcamp.com)

Take Off
Recommended surf lessons from one hour to two weeks. The owner runs the Master of the Ocean competition. (321takeoff.com)

19 Diving in SOSÚA

BEACHES | DIVING | NIGHTLIFE

Though just 14km from Cabarete, the neighboring beach town of Sosúa offers a distinctly different vibe. Trade in the high-energy thrill of water sports for a slower pace where it's lazing on beaches by day and raucous nightlife after dark. It's also the diving hub of the North Coast, with local dive operators running trips to dive sites around Sosúa Bay.

How To

Getting here and around A short 8km jaunt from the airport, Sosúa is centrally located to many of the North Coast's towns and highlights.

When to go Year-round, but the less rainy months from November to February offer the best beach weather.

Top tip If you're coming here to do your PADI, get a head start by doing the eLearning theory online (and possibly even the pool skills) to save time becoming certified on your holiday.

Under the sea While the North Coast is most associated with catching wild rides kiteboarding and surfing, below the ocean's surface there's just as much adventure awaiting. Sosúa is the go-to place for diving and snorkeling, with some of the Caribbean's best dives, ranging from shallow 14m reefs to deep 53m drop-offs. Expect vibrant soft corals, schools of tropical fish and wreck dives including the *Zíngara,* a 45m-long ship sunk in 1993 to create an artificial reef in about 35m of water. Recommended operators that run trips and certification

Right Bluehead wrasse, Sosúa

ROB ATHERTON/ALAMY

courses include **Superior Dive** (superiordivesosua.com), **Sosua Diving Center** (sosuadivingcenter.com) and, further afield, **Blue Tang Divers** (divingpuertoplata.com) in Costa Dorada.

Life's a beach Feasting on seafood with a cold juice, beer or cocktail in hand and your toes in the sand is what Caribbean holiday legends are made of. And what Sosúa lacks in water sports, it makes up for with palm-fringed white-sand beaches. Vibey **Playa Sosúa** is its main beach, a pretty crescent-shaped patch of sand with a fun, lively, local atmosphere – especially on Sundays when boom boxes blare merengue – that's popular with Dominican families. Beach shacks serve up fried fish and lobster, and there's snorkeling gear to hire so you can swim the reef among tropical fish. Midweek is much more chilled. Nearby, the lovely white sands of little **Playa Alicia** make for a more relaxed alternative to Sosúa.

Further afield Two adjacent beaches of **Playa Dorada** and **Costa Dorada** are both stunning options a few kilometers east of Puerto Plata.

Sosúa's Jewish Heritage

The beach resort town of Sosúa has an interesting past as the location where some 750 Jewish refugees landed in 1940 after fleeing Nazi persecution in Germany. The DR was the only country to officially accept Jewish refugees, ironically as part of Trujillo's efforts to 'whiten' the country's population. Here they established the dairy industry (still going strong today), and you can learn about their story at the **Museo de la Comunidad Judía de Sosúa** (sosuajewishmuseum.com). Next door is the original synagogue that's still used today as a place of worship by descendants of Jewish-Dominican settlers.

20 LEAP into Waterfalls

JUNGLE | CANYONING | SWIMMING

For those wanting to dive headfirst into a fully immersive jungle adventure, take the plunge, literally, at 27 Waterfalls of Damajagua. Just south of Puerto Plata, this popular wet-and-wild day trip will have you leaping off waterfalls into natural pools in between canyoning through rivers, sliding down rocky water slides and traversing rainforest trails.

AGENCJA FOTOGRAFICZNA CARO/ALAMY

How To

Getting here Located inland 33km southwest of Puerto Plata. If on a tour, transportation is included; otherwise, rent a car or take a local bus from Puerto Plata (30 minutes) or Santiago (one hour).

When to go Rainier months (June to August) are more scenic; drier months (November to March) more accessible.

Avoid the crowds Get here as early as you can to avoid cruise-ship day-trippers.

Info 27waterfalls.org

MAURITIUS IMAGES GMBH/ALAMY

SANTIAGO VIDAL VALLEJO_LAMY

Bottom left Waterfall and swimming hole, 27 Waterfalls of Damajagua **Top left** Hikers on stairs to one of the falls **Left** Final pool, 27 Waterfalls of Damajagua

27 Waterfalls of Damajagua The most popular day trip on the North Coast, this fun-filled excursion mixes pristine nature with adrenaline as you jump into a series of sparkling clear pools deep in the rainforest. After a sweaty 30-minute walk through the jungle, there's no better way to cool off than leaping like a lemming into refreshing natural pools. You'll then splash your way through the limestone-carved river on foot, taking rock slides en route to the next jump – the highest is 8m. If that all sounds too action-packed, those who don't want to jump can take the stairs. Though there are 27 'waterfalls' (which are actually pools), only seven or so are accessible due to drought and trees blocking the path.

Tours and guides Guides, who can be contracted upon arrival, are mandatory. Otherwise, sign up for a tour. **Kayak River Adventures** (kayakriveradventures.com) in Cabarete is recommended, and also offers other canyoning trips for those wanting something more challenging. Life jackets and helmets are provided, but bring water, sunscreen, waterproofing for your phone and closed-toe water shoes (available to hire on arrival).

Zip and dip If you're seeking more thrills, add zip-lining into the mix. Climb to the 12th waterfall, then speed down via a succession of five zip lines and two suspension bridges to reach the seventh falls. From here you'll dive into the canyon among the falls.

The Legend of Damajagua

Long before the falls were 'discovered' for tourism in the 1990s, Damajagua held deep spiritual significance for the Taínos, who believed the waterfalls were a sacred meeting place for nature's spirits. According to legend, the falls were named after Damajagua, the son of a Taíno chief, who discovered them during his explorations and fell in love with Yara, daughter of Boinayel, the god of rain. Boinayel forbade their love and struck Damajagua with lightning, but Yara stepped in to take the blow and died. Grief-stricken, Damajagua leapt to his death. Boinayel, remorseful, wept – his tears forming more falls and carving their *cemíes* (Taíno spirits) into the rocks you see today.

21 CULTURAL Puerto Plata

AMBER | MUSEUMS | HISTORY

Sure, the palm-fringed beaches and water adventures draw visitors to the North Coast, but don't miss picturesque Puerto Plata. Its pastel-hued colonial-era streets, rich history and golden amber, showcased in museums and galleries, make it a cultural gem.

OLEKSANDRA IABLOCHKOVA/GETTY IMAGES

How To

Getting here Aeropuerto Internacional Gregorio Luperón is 18km east of town. A taxi to the airport costs US$35; otherwise, walk 500m to the main highway to flag down a *guagua* to Puerto Plata (45 minutes).

When to go February for the color and energy of Carnival.

Did you know? The mosquito embedded in amber in Museo del Ámbar Dominicano features in the opening scenes of *Jurassic Park*.

TOMMY TRENCHARD/ALAMY

Romancing in the Stone

One could be forgiven for thinking the 'Amber Coast' earned its moniker from the golden sands of the northern beaches. Instead, it owes the title to the region's rich deposits of amber, particularly around Puerto Plata. The best place to explore this captivating fossilized resin – which often contains trappings of species millions of years old – is **Museo del Ámbar Dominicano** (ambermuseum.com). Housed in an elegant Victorian-era building, the museum offers guided tours that trace amber's journey from sticky resin to gemstone – exploring how it forms, how it's extracted from replica mines 100m deep, and how it's polished to reveal its luminous, honeyed glow. Prized specimens exhibited include Jurassic-era flora, ancient insects, a 50-million-year-old lizard and an exquisite

MARK PITT IMAGES/SHUTTERSTOCK

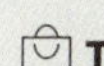

The Finer Things

Macorix House of Rum Get the lowdown on rum production before sampling the goods. (macorixhouseofrum.com/en; tour US$8)

Del Oro A chocolate factory bean-to-bar experience with plenty of tastings. (facebook.com/delorochocolate)

Espigón Cigar Factory Drop in to see how handmade premium cigars are rolled. (@espigoncigar)

Left Museo del Ámbar Dominicano
Top left Puerto Plata street
Above Fossilized fly in amber

30cm-long feather preserved in amber. The museum also explores another iconic Dominican export: tobacco. With an onsite cigar factory operated by La Aurora – the country's oldest cigar maker (p189) – visitors can watch the production process and even light up to sample the goods. For additional insights, stop by **Galería de Ambar** (amber collection.itgo.com) covering amber, tobacco, rum, sugar and coffee production.

Forts & Museums

While you won't find anything as ancient as 50-million-year-old amber, Puerto Plata's old town offers fascinating glimpses into its past. Wander through the **Centro Histórico de Puerto Plata**, where ornate Victorian-era mansions once housed wealthy landowners and merchants, before arriving at **Fuerte de San Felipe** (adult RD$100, kids under 8 free), one of the oldest colonial-era structures in the Caribbean. Built in 1577 from limestone, this

Scenic Drive

For a scenic road trip into rural Dominican life, take the winding **Ruta Panorámica** from Puerto Plata to Santiago. This 30km mountain route climbs through the Cordillera Septentrional, reaching 800m above sea level, with sweeping views of lush hills, farms and villages. A key stop is **La Cumbre**, home to the world's largest **amber mines** – famous for rare blue amber. If you're thinking of buying from a miner, note foreigners can't export raw amber, so pick up polished pieces from nearby workshops instead. The route also passes a poignant monument marking where political dissidents the Mirabal sisters were murdered – an act that helped spark the fall of the dictator Trujillo.

Left Centro Histórico de Puerto Plata
Below Fuerte de San Felipe

Spanish fort defended one of the few sheltered bays from pirate raids. Perched at the western end of the Malecón, its hilltop location offers stunning Atlantic views. The audio tour guides you through its role in the 1800 Quasi War, when it was seized by the US Navy without a shot being fired. The small museum displays rusty shackles, bayonets, coins and cannonballs in a space formerly used as prison cells – including infamously during Trujillo's regime when one of the DR's founding fathers, Juan Pablo Duarte, was detained here.

Continue along the coastal path to the restored 19th-century **lighthouse**, standing 24.4m tall in neoclassical-industrial style, on a walk that stretches 2km along the coastal **Malecón**.

Another must-visit is the **Casa Museo General Gregorio Luperón** (facebook.com/Museo.Gregorio.Luperon; adult/child RD$200/100). Set in a beautifully preserved Victorian home, it celebrates the life of national hero Gregorio Luperón (1839–97), who was born and died in Puerto Plata. The museum's eight rooms display personal belongings, documents and artifacts that tell the story of Luperón's pivotal role in the Dominican Restoration War, which led to the country's independence from Spain in 1865.

22 LAID-BACK Río San Juan

BEACHES | SNORKELING | SURFING

Just an hour east of tourist hot spot Cabarete, the laid-back town of Río San Juan offers a low-key alternative for those seeking beaches, surfing and snorkeling. The main draw is its gateway to a dreamy coastline of beautiful palm-fringed beaches and crystal-clear waters, up there with the best in the DR.

TRAVELSTOCK44/ALAMY

How To

Getting here Buses connect Río San Juan with Santo Domingo (3½ hours); *guaguas* run to Cabarete (1½ hours), Sosúa (1½ hours) and Puerto Plata (two hours).

When to go Winter (December to February) offers great beach weather but attracts crowds; visit during the shoulder seasons for fewer tourists.

Take care Playa Grande is prone to strong, powerful waves, in which case it's best to avoid swimming. Drownings occur, so be sure you know what to do if caught in a rip.

ARIELFI HERNANDEZ POLANCO/SHUTTERSTOCK

A great alternative to the mega resorts of Punta Cana, Río San Juan offers a laid-back escape with a lineup of beaches to suit every mood: rugged surf spots, family-friendly bays, and secluded coves.

Town beaches In town, tiny, delightful **Playa Los Mino** is one of the DR's most enticing urban beaches, offering a slice of localized Caribbean family fun. Just north, peaceful **Playa de Los Guardias** is perfect for kids and snorkelers with its shallow, calm, crystal-clear waters.

Playa Caletón About 1km northeast, Playa Caletón is another family favorite – a superb crescent bay with soft white sand and calm waters ideal for snorkeling and lounging.

Playa Grande Then comes the granddaddy of the North Coast, Playa Grande, considered one of the DR's most stunning beaches. Spanning 2km, it offers something for everyone – from its lively sections with beach chairs, umbrellas, surf schools and seafood shacks to its long, quiet western stretch.

Further afield A short stroll east lies **Playa Preciosa** ('Precious Beach'), a smaller, quieter beach that lives up to its name and is favored by surfers. Further east, **Playa El Bretón** has sparkling waters ideal for snorkeling, while **Playa La Entrada** offers a wild, remote stretch of beach that's often blissfully empty on weekdays and livelier on weekends when local food and drink stalls open up.

Bottom left Playa Los Mino
Top left Playa Grande

Laguna Dudú

Just a 31km drive from Río San Juan, **Laguna Dudú** is a series of cenotes with crystal-clear waters popular for swimming, snorkeling and kayaking in a lush, tropical setting. Adventurers can zip-line into the lagoon, plunging straight into its cool spring-fed waters. Known as one of the top freshwater cavern dives in the Caribbean, visibility can reach up to 50m, though diving is currently off-limits due to safety concerns since the tragic deaths of two Italian divers in 2022. Snorkelers can still enjoy spotting fish and rock formations. While natural, the area has been developed with steps and platforms. Arrive early to enjoy the experience before the crowds arrive, especially on weekends.

23 ESCAPE to the Country

HIKING | MOUNTAINS | WATERFALLS

Of course, the golden beaches of the North Coast are stunning, but venture inland and discover a different kind of beauty. Nature lovers will be captivated by Tubagua Ecolodge, a mountain retreat offering all-encompassing vistas, scenic hiking and a place to unwind amid rural life in the stunning Cordillera Septentrional mountain range.

MAURITIUS IMAGES GMBH/ALAMY

How To

Getting here A mere 25-minute drive from Puerto Plata, this region is accessed via the inland Rte 25 that links up with Santiago (42km).

When to go Year-round, but mid-season hurricane months (June to October) are possibly best avoided.

Keep an eye out for Birders looking to tick off unique species can aim for the narrow-billed and the broad-billed todies, both endemic to the area.

MAURITIUS IMAGES GMBH/ALAMY

MAURITIUS IMAGES GMBH/ALAMY

Bottom left Hikers jumping into a [illegible] Cordillera Septentrional **Top left** View across Cordillera Septentrional **Left** Tubagua Ecolodge

Inland treasures Swap your beach towel for hiking boots and head to the hills just 25 minutes inland from Puerto Plata to **Tubagua Ecolodge** (tubagua.com). Nestled in the central highlands, this rustic retreat features open-air, thatched-roof bungalows with sweeping views of verdant countryside and the Atlantic Ocean. Wake up to magical sunrises right from your bed. Unwind in hammocks scattered across breezy, flower-filled gardens or soak up the sun by the pool. Even if you're not staying overnight, the onsite restaurant is worth a visit for hearty Dominican dishes paired with panoramic mountain vistas. Plus, 10% of its income supports a local food program.

Get out among it For an authentic taste of rural Dominican life, join one of Tubagua's **nature treks** led by friendly English-speaking guides. Owner Tim Hall – who also serves as the Canadian Honorary Consul in Puerto Plata – shares deep insight into the region's culture, ecology and sustainable tourism practices. Along the way, you'll explore farms and meadows, learning about the local ecosystem and centuries-old traditions, before arriving at 'God's Swimming Pool' – a crystal-clear spring feeding a series of stunning natural cascades.

You can also visit a nearby organic coffee plantation, where you'll learn all about the full bean-to-cup process and enjoy a fresh brew.

A Slower Pace

After living here for 40 years, people say the Dominican Republic must have changed a lot. But up here around the lodge, things have hardly changed at all. Tubagua Ecolodge is part of a country village on top of a mountain, about 19km (12 miles) from Puerto Plata. From the vast ocean view out in front, to the thick forests and lush farmland, to the small-town congeniality of our neighbors, Tubagua feels as authentic and natural as when we first moved here in 1984. And while the big cities are now jammed with cars, condos and fast-food chains, the local customs and the way of life in our tiny country town nurture our appreciation for a simple, happy existence, for the way we were.

Tim Hall, *owner, Tubagua Ecolodge*

24 Step Back IN TIME

HISTORY | VIEWS | BEACHES

Parque Nacional La Isabela marks the spot where Christopher Columbus landed on his second voyage in 1493, founding one of the first European settlements in the Americas. This historic site also serves as a somber reminder of colonization's toll – the enslavement and destruction of the Taínos and Macorix, whose cultures were forever altered by European conquest.

DMITRY CHULOV/SHUTTERSTOCK

How To

Getting here and around Parque Nacional La Isabela is located 42km west of Puerto Plata. A taxi from Luperón, 11km to the east, will set you back US$50 return (if the driver waits) and a *motoconcho* around RD$200 one way.

When to go Year-round, but drier months (December to March) are ideal; aim to arrive in the morning before it gets too hot.

Don't forget Bring your swimsuit and towel as there are beaches out this way, too.

DMITRY CHULOV/SHUTTERSTOCK

HACKENBERG-PHOTO-COLOGNE/ALAMY

Bottom left Plaque at the ruins of La Isabela **Top left** Graves of the first residents of La Isabela settlement **Left** Templo de las Américas

Parque Nacional La Isabela Although it was the Vikings who established the first European settlement in the Americas around 1000 CE, it was short-lived and abandoned – so fast-forward nearly 500 years, when Christopher Columbus' first voyage from Spain led to the establishment of the fort La Navidad in Hispaniola (near modern Cap-Haïtien in Haiti) in 1492. But upon Columbus' return the next year, he found it burnt to the ground, which duly led to the creation of **La Isabela**, 110km east, in 1493: the first permanent European settlement in the Americas. On the tentative list of UNESCO World Heritage Sites, today this 2-hectare site is protected as part of the Parque Nacional La Isabela, which comprises archaeological ruins that are perched on a scenic bluff overlooking the azure waters of the Atlantic Ocean.

Ruins and replicas Included with your entrance ticket is a 30-minute guided tour of La Isabela's **archaeological site**, which features the rudimentary foundations of several oceanfront buildings, a cemetery (with a replica skeleton of a Spanish soldier) and the remnants of the original settlement. A small **museum** (admission RD$100) displays exhibits about the Taínos, old coins, arrowheads and a model of Columbus' house – the only place in the Americas where he lived. Across from the park stands the **Templo de las Américas**, a 1994 replica of La Isabela's original church, commemorating the settlement's 500th anniversary.

La Isabela was abandoned after three years due to disease and other struggles, with the settlement moving to Nueva Isabela (now Santo Domingo) in 1498.

Taíno Genocide

Columbus' second voyage in 1493, often hailed as the 'founding' of the Americas, brought 17 ships and over 1500 settlers. For the indigenous peoples of Hispaniola, it marked the beginning of devastation. The Taíno and Macorix were enslaved, displaced and subjected to cultural erasure. European diseases like smallpox and measles, against which they had no immunity, decimated their populations. By the mid-1500s, up to 90% of the indigenous populaton had vanished. Despite this, traces of Taíno culture endure today through language, traditions and spiritual practices, a testament to their resilience in the face of cultural destruction.

Listings

BEST OF THE REST

Cabarete Cafe Culture

Cabarete Coffee Company $

All-day breakfasts span from fruit with cacao to fully loaded burritos. The highlight is the organic, homegrown coffee. Proceeds go toward empowering local girls in the community.

Vagamundo Coffee & Waffles $

The name of this popular cafe says it all: single-origin coffees and mind-blowing gourmet waffles. Also brings in the brunch crowd for hearty, healthy protein and smoothie bowls.

Belgium Bakery $

Swap beach views for a shady terrace at this long-time fave serving full-cooked English breakfasts, omelets, pastries and strong coffee. Has Belgium chocolates, too, along with burgers and beers for later in the day.

Panadería & Repostería Dick $

Perfect for hangovers or post-water workouts is this German bakery serving carb-heavy breakfasts of house-baked breads with cold cuts, eggs, cheese and strong coffee.

Fresh Fresh Café $$

Cool, cozy and super-chilled cafe with a menu that's all about light, healthy and delicious organic fare made from scratch. Expect tasty loaded health bowls and nutrient-boosting smoothies.

Cabarete Beach Views

Wilson La Boca Restaurant $

Located in Islabon, 8km southeast of Cabarete, is this rustic waterfront shack cooking up divine wood-fired barbecue fish, chicken and lobster enjoyed on the sandy banks of Río Yasica.

El Cocotazo Cafe $

Overlooking all the action at Kite Beach, watch kiteboaders do their thing while tucking into fish tacos, burgers and sunset beers and cocktails. All-day breakfasts and happy-hour drink specials (4pm to 5pm).

Front Loop Café & Grill $$

If you've come to the DR for magnificent seafood and beach views (and who hasn't?), Front Loop delivers on both fronts: whole grilled snapper, mahi-mahi in coconut sauce and azure ocean vistas.

Pomodoro $$

Life doesn't get much better than wood-fired pizzas on the sand alongside homemade pastas, gelato and happy-hour cocktails.

La Casita de Papi $$$

Beachfront institution where you can dine on delicious lobster and grilled fish with sand between your toes. Come evenings its fairy-lit ambience ensues romance aplenty.

IMAGE PROFESSIONALS GMBH/ALAMY

La Casita de Papi

NORTH COAST REVIEWS

Velero Sunset Grill $$$

Head to Velero Beach Resort on its namesake beach to watch stunning sunsets while dining on fresh seafood. A great spot to sample Dominican cuisine, including Caribbean crab cakes, lobster dishes and seared fresh tuna.

Cabarete Drinks

Mojito Bar

Come during the day to enjoy the beach views and tasty food, and in the evenings not just for its namesake minty rum cocktails, but icy daiquiris blended with fresh local fruits.

Voyvoy

Chilled beach bar with a menu of burgers and beers. In the evenings, it morphs into a dance party with DJs spinning tracks or more relaxed bands from Thursdays to Saturdays.

LAX Ojo

Atmospheric beachfront restaurant at the eastern end of Playa Cabarete that opens late for parties, DJs and live music.

Cabarete Inland Restaurants

Gordito's Fresh Mex $$

The North Coast's best Tex-Mex is famous for its mouthwatering Mambo fish taco wrapped in a flour tortilla, a burrito or bowl. Other favorites include the chipotle shrimp and 'Big Mac' burrito.

Bliss $$$

One to dress up for is this romantic restaurant with white-linen tablecloths set around a sparkling pool. The menu of Caribbean and Mediterranean cuisine is paired with quality wines and a long list of cocktails.

Blue Moon $$$

Reserve ahead for dinner at this mountain eco-retreat, a short drive from Cabarete, serving quality three-course Indian-Caribbean

TRAVELSTOCK44/ALAMY

Voyvoy

fusion using local produce and organic vegetables grown onsite.

Sosúa Eats

Waterfront Playa Alicia Restaurant $$

Kick back with a piña colada to take in dreamy ocean views while feasting on a menu that varies from Dominican stews and coconut-battered grouper to grilled meats and American classics.

Taberna El Conde $$

Away from the beach is this old Sosúa tourist haunt offering a varied menu of daily specials such as cottage pie, tacos and curries. Good spot for a drink, too.

Michael's Stone Bar $$

At the southern end of Playa Sosúa is this clifftop seafood restaurant offering amazing views accompanied by grilled whole sea bass or snapper paired with cold beers or refreshing mojitos.

Mofongo King $

This open-air beachside seafood restaurant on Playa Sosúa does a menu of coastal classics: cold beer, fried fish and cheese burgers, alongside its signature *mofongo* (mashed plantains with pork rind).

Raise a Glass in Sosúa

Bailees

Part of the Sosua Inn Hotel, this Caribbean restaurant offers both Dominican and international dishes. Its newly opened Sky Lounge Bar is a swanky choice for evening cocktails.

Blue Ice Piano Bar

No tinkling of the ivories here – just DJs and thumping beats. Perfect if you're looking to party, but be aware of Sosúa's reputation for its seedy nightlife.

North Coast Brewers

Craft-beer lovers rejoice: Sosúa has a taproom doing an interesting array of ales produced onsite – from IPAs and German beers to red blonde and seasonal ales. Onsite food and an ax-throwing gallery, too!

More to See in Puerto Plata

Teleférico

The Teleférico's 800m cable car ride up Pico Isabel de Torres offers sweeping views, botanical gardens, caves and the iconic Christ the Redeemer statue.

Calle de las Sombrillas

Come by this Instagrammable alley known as 'Umbrella Street,' with a canopy decorated in multicolored umbrellas, along with vibrant murals, cafes, ice cream and buskers.

Paseo de Doña Blanca

Vibrant, photogenic pink alley just off Parque Central honoring Bianca Franceschini, an Italian who settled in Puerto Plata in 1898.

Puerto Plata Dining & Drinking

Kaffe $

For old-world ambience head to Puerto Plata's Centro Histórico for hearty breakfasts, iced coffees or cocktails at this Victorian-era house that's been converted into a cafe.

Restaurant Pizzeria SoleMio $

Just west of Puerto Plata in Costambar is this expat go-to for authentic Italian cuisine with wood-fired pizza cooked in a stone oven, homemade pastas and sauces.

El Farolito $$

Life here truly is a beach. With tables on the sands of Playa Costambar, enjoy cold beers and fried fish at this family-run restaurant.

La Carihuela Beach $$

Catch a sea breeze at this beachside bistro along the Malecón doing fresh seafood and delicious churrasco. Good spot for mojitos and margaritas, and weekends get going with DJs and live merengue.

Le Petit François $$

For a rollicking good time, head east to Playa Doara. At this beachfront beauty it's all about lobster, piña coladas and Dominican, French and French Canadian favorites like poutine.

More Adventure & Activities

Parque Nacional Monte Cristi

Escape the crowds at this seldom-visited park surrounding the town of Monte Cristi; 1100

MY.MIRACLE.BOX/SHUTTERSTOCK

Paseo de Doña Blanca

sq km of wonderful desertscapes, beautiful beaches and treks up El Morro (239m) for stunning views.

Parque Nacional El Choco

Just south of Cabarete is this swath of verdant wilderness most known for its caves. Privately owned, they're visited on a 1½ hour tour (US$20 admission). Don't forget your swimsuit for the crystal-clear pools.

Rancho El Contento

Escape Cabarete's beach scene and ride through stunning mountains on horseback. Led by a horse-loving German guide, half- and full-day tours include villages, mountains and beach rides.

Kayak River Adventures

Canyoning and rappelling tours (and courses) to lesser-visited sites at the 27 Falls, including places named Magic Mushroom and Big Bastard. It also offers half- and full-day kayak and SUP tours.

Sosua Game Fishing

Reel in a big one on these chartered deep-fishing tours based in Playa Sosúa. Offers half- and full-day trips, before heading back to its clubhouse to cook up your catch.

Cabarete Language Institute

¿No hablas español? Gringos looking to step up their language game can learn conversational Spanish here, with one-on-one or group lessons.

Eric Tours

Reliable, Sosúa-based tour company covering most bases: SUP rentals, guided trips, zip-lining, jungle excursions, party boat trips and more.

MATYAS REHAK/SHUTTERSTOCK

Parque Nacional El Choco

Monkey Jungle

On the edge of Parque Nacional El Choco is the DR's longest zip-line park, stretching over 1370m across seven stations. Proceeds go to nonprofit HADAC (hadac.org), assisting with local medical care.

Eating Out in Río San Juan

La Casita de Playa $

In a prime location on the white sands of Playa Los Mino, this rustic seafood shack's temptations of lobster, cold beers and piña coladas are hard to resist.

La Casona $

Good spot to indulge in home-style Dominican delights, including what is many people's vote for the DR's best empanada. Don't miss the crispy crab-filled variety.

Café de Paris $$

Overlooking Laguna Gri-Gri is this French bistro doing coffee, crepes and croissants alongside heartier dishes and a good selection of fresh juices and cocktails.

CENTRAL HIGHLANDS

MOUNTAINS | AGRICULTURE | ADVENTURE

CENTRAL HIGHLANDS

Trip Builder

Beyond the oh-so-real Caribbean cliché of beaches and palm trees, the superb lush interior of DR's Central Highlands await. Here you'll hike summits, raft rivers and let loose at Carnival in between savoring premium cigars, coffee and organic chocolate in what's an adventurous, fun-packed region.

Feel the rhythm of **merengue** at its birthplace in Santiago (p186)
1¼hr from Puerto Plata

Scale the Caribbeans's highest peak, **Pico Duarte** (p174)
1hr from Jarabacoa

FROM LEFT: MARIELA ELIZABETH PERALTA/SHUTTERSTOCK, NURPHOTO/GETTY IMAGES, MATYAS REHAK/SHUTTERSTOCK, PREVIOUS SPREAD: PASS_TRAL/SHUTTERSTOCK

Practicalities

KOBBYMENDEZ/SHUTTERSTOCK

ARRIVING

Aeropuerto Internacionál del Cibao If you're arriving via Santiago's airport, it's around a one- or two-hour bus ride to the Cordillera Central's main attractions.

Caribe Tours From Santo Domingo, there are buses to both Santiago and Jarabacoa (2½ hours).

HOW MUCH FOR A

Rafting tour US$60

Cigar US$3–10

Merengue class US$30

WHEN TO GO

FEB
Carnival is in full swing in towns like La Vega and Santiago.

APR–JUN
Shoulder season means less people and lower costs, but weather's a mixed bag.

JUN–NOV
Traditional hurricane season can bring wet weather, but it's generally dry around Santiago.

NOV–APR
Peak season for climbing Pico Duarte. Baseball season through to January.

GETTING AROUND

Guagua These local buses are good for short jaunts within towns and for onward journeys. Flag them down by the highway.

Car Self-drive is the most practical option in the Central Highlands, but the lack of streetlights, potholed roads, non-signposted one-way streets and reckless drivers sharing narrow streets can be challenging.

Taxi Flagging down a *motoconcho* (motorcycle taxi) is a handy option for shorter journeys. There's Uber in the cities, but in rural mountain towns like Jarabacoa, you'll hail a taxi instead.

EATING & DRINKING

Santiago is home to a flourishing epicurean scene with a good mix of local and upmarket cuisine. The fertile soils of the Ciabao region are the breadbasket of the country, so expect plenty of fresh, local produce, including quality organic coffee and cacao that you can sample on farm tours. For traditional dishes, head to open-air *comedores* (eateries) for *La Bandera* (colorful plate of rice, red beans and stewed meat), *mofongo* (mashed plantains with fried pork rinds) and *mangú* (mashed green plantains; pictured bottom right) for breakfast.

Best Dominican cuisine
Camp David (p196)

Must-try chocolate
Sendero del Cacao (p193)

CONNECT & FIND YOUR WAY

Wi-fi You'll find wi-fi in most accommodations throughout the region, though you'll likely lose signal in the national parks on treks.

Navigation Maps.me is a good app for offline navigation, both on foot and if driving. With that said, guides are compulsory for most treks, so getting lost shouldn't be a problem.

WHERE TO STAY

In the Central Highlands you'll find a good choice of accommodations within your budget and tastes: from charming hotels in Santiago to campsites in rural mountain regions.

Place	Pros/Cons
Santiago	This transit hub offers a reasonable array of options. Bookings required for Carnival.
Jarabacoa	Best sleeping options are just outside town along the Río Yaque del Norte. Budget travelers are well catered for.
Constanza	A good base for trips into the mountains and waterfalls. Mostly modest, small family-run hotels. Things get busy on weekends.
La Vega	The only reason to visit is for Carnival. Sleeping options aren't overly inspired.

PACK THAT JACKET

If you were umming and ahhing about whether to pack warm clothing for your holiday, for those coming to the Central Highlands, it's a definite yes!

MONEY

Keeping things local is the best way to keep costs down: using *guaguas* and eating in *comedores* will save you money.

25 Thrills & SPILLS

RAFTING | CANYONING | GLIDING

Sitting in the foothills of the Cordillera Central, Jarabacoa draws thrill-seekers to tame rapids, leap down waterfalls and soar through the skies. Take a walk on the wild side and dive into the adventure capital of the 'Dominican Alps.'

NICK HANNA/ALAMY

How To

Getting here and around Buses run to Jarabacoa from Santo Domingo (two hours) via La Vega (45 minutes), where you can transfer to Santiago (40 minutes). Take a *motoconcho* or cab to get around town.

When to go Year-round but the drier months (December to April) are more pleasant without the rain.

Seeking more hard-core thrills? Inquire with Rancho Baiguate about Río Yaque del Norte's Class IV and V rapids.

HEMIS/ALAMY

River Rafting

Strap on your helmet and life jacket, and grab a paddle to conquer the Yaque del Norte, the Caribbean's longest – and only raftable – river. On this thrilling 1½-hour adventure, you'll tackle roaring Class II and III rapids with names like Mike Tyson and the Cemetery – indicators of the wild ride ahead! Between the adrenaline rushes, enjoy calm stretches as you kick back and enjoy the scenic canyon views. Recommended tour operators include **Rancho Baiguate** (ranchobaiguate.com) and **Jaraventura** (jaraventura.com).

Canyoning

Though this is a region blessed with splendid waterfalls, it's only here in Jarabacoa where you get right among them on an epic canyoning tour in the tropical wilderness of

TRAVELSTUFF/SHUTTERSTOCK

Riding Rapids

Rafting in Jarabacoa connects me with nature and releases my adrenaline. The Yaque del Norte Río challenges me with its lively current, while the green mountains embrace each descent. I love it, because with each wave I discover a new emotion and feel completely alive, free and happy.

Victor Garrido, *rafting guide @jaraventura*

Left View from El Mogote (p171)
Top left White-water rafting near Jarabacoa
Above Canyoning down a waterfall

the Caribbean, a thrilling adventure rappelling 30m cascades in between traversing and leaping into river beds and zip-line crossings. There are a few operators in town; otherwise, Rancho Baiguate and Jaraventura remain reliable choices. This could well be the most adrenaline-fueled day of your trip.

A Bird's-Eye View

If you're still looking for a bigger high, then **Flying Tony** is your man. This long-standing paragliding operator will take you to the skies for a tandem ride over what are unquestionably the best views (and adrenaline rush) in the DR. Here you'll glide like an eagle while being treated to spectacular topographical views over the Central Highlands mountains, rivers and valleys.

Mountain Biking

There's plenty of two-wheel action here too, with the **Tri Mountain MTB Park**

Something More Chilled?

If you want to soak in the beauty of the mountains without flinging yourself off waterfalls or tackling multi-day treks to remote peaks, there's plenty of gentler outdoor fun to enjoy.

Tubing Float lazily down the Yaque del Norte on tubing tours, letting the current carry you while you take in the scenery.

Horseback riding Meander through lush forests on horseback, a peaceful way to experience the landscape.

Massage Relax with a restorative massage, pool time and sauna at **Akasha Spa**, surrounded by nature's sounds.

Social swim Join locals at **Balneario La Confluencia** for a Sunday swim and picnic where two rivers meet.

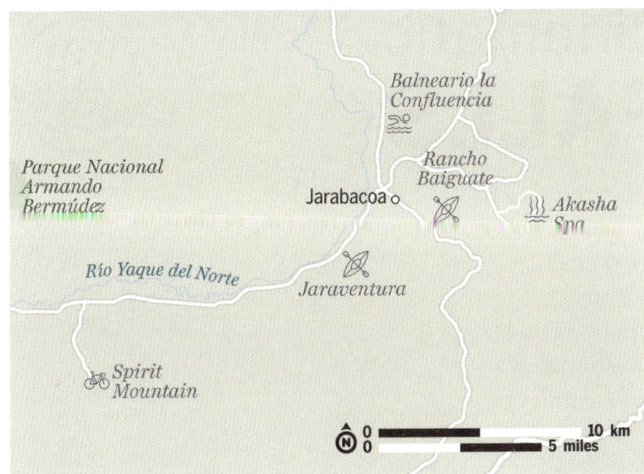

Left Paragliding, Jarabacoa
Below View over Cordillera Central mountains

(day pass RD$300) offering the best option for mountain-bike riders in what is the DR's first purpose-built, downhill single trail. It was set up by the folk at **Spirit Mountain**, and is a thrilling ride through the scenic forest with plenty of jumps and technical features – suitable for beginners to advanced riders.

For something cruisier, sign up for an e-bike tour with Jaraventura to navigate steep gradients without breaking into a sweat as you visit its falls, natural pools and coffee plantations.

Hiking

Though it doesn't reach the lofty heights of Pico Duarte (p174), **El Mogote** (1573m) is a popular summit just west of town. To reach the trailhead 5km away, hop in a taxi (around RD$200 one-way). The steep, three- to four-hour climb follows a poorly maintained, often slippery trail – best suited for experienced hikers. Hiring an English-speaking guide through Jaraventura is recommended; they'll point out the area's impressive biodiversity, from pine forests and birdlife to panoramic views over the Jarabacoa Valley, Yaque del Norte and Pico Duarte. Start early, wear proper hiking boots and pack plenty of water, food and supplies. **Spirit Mountain** also offers scenic forest trails through its coffee plantation, perfect for bird-watching.

26 Cinematic FALLS

CASCADES | JUNGLE | SWIMMING

Jarabacoa offes easy access to some of the Dominican Republic's most spectacular waterfalls, all surrounded by roaring rivers, lush canyons and forested hillsides. Making for a popular day trip, highlights include Salto de Jimenoa Uno and, further afield, Aguas Blancas, one of the country's highest falls, best visited on the scenic drive to Constanza.

How To

Getting here Jarabacoa's three main waterfalls are 6km to 10km from town, well-signed off the main road. Trailheads are easily reached by car, with up to an hour's walk. *Motoconchos* cost about RD$500 return.

When to go Year-round but dry season (December to March) is less slippery and less muddy. Conversely, wet season has a greater flow of water.

Avoid Do not swim under the falls. This is a big no-no, and sadly several deaths have occurred.

Salto de Jimenoa Uno Featured briefly in *Jurassic Park*, Salto de Jimenoa Uno is the largest and most scenic of Jarabacoa's waterfalls. Water cascades 60m through a hole in the rock face into a clear pool. It's a sweaty 20-minute hike through lush forest to reach it, but as tempting as it is to swim, it's dangerous under the falls themselves and fatalities have occurred. For safer swimming, head to Baiguate.

Salto de Jimenoa Dos Often just called Salto de Jimenoa (just to confuse things...), this very popular 40m cascade recently reopened after bridge

Right Salto de Jimenoa Uno

DENIS KABANOV/SHUTTERSTOCK

repairs. It's a 600m walk from the parking lot through jungle trails and suspension bridges crossing the Río Jimenoa. Swimming is allowed at designated river areas, but not directly under the falls.

Salto de Baiguate Located 5km south of town, Baiguate isn't the tallest but it's the go-to spot for swimming. Brace yourself, however, as it's cold! It's a short, steep 10-minute hike down, and is also a popular destination for horseback treks.

Salto de Aguas Blancas Saving the best for last, this stunner crashes down 135m over three sections. Salto de Aguas Blancas lies 60km south near Constanza. Set among pine forests at 1680m altitude, it's the Caribbean's highest waterfall. Bring your swimsuit, but the water is freezing! If you're not on a tour, you'll need a 4WD to access here. From the car park it's 25-minute walk through jungle.

A Caribbean Shangri La

If you're planning to pack only swimsuits and summer clothes for the Dominican Republic, think again. At 1283m, the beautiful, Shangri La–like town of **Constanza** sits in a meteorite-formed crater in the heart of the Cordillera Central, making it one of the country's chilliest spots. Just a 45-minute drive south of Jarabacoa, this fertile 'breadbasket' town offers a peaceful alternative base for exploring Aguas Blancas, climbing Pico Duarte and heading out to adventure sports sights. Nearby, you'll find Taíno petroglyphs at **Piedras Letradas**, lush trails at **Reserva Científica Ebano Verde** and the remote **Reserva Científica Valle Nuevo** – the country's coldest region at 2438m.

Scaling Pico DUARTE

PEAKS | NATURE | TREKKING

The possibility of scaling Pico Duarte is one that lures 'peak baggers' from far and wide, hoping to tick off the Caribbean's highest mountain. At 3098m, it's a strenuous trek taking anywhere from two to five days, and is best suited for experienced, physically fit trekkers.

MAURITIUS IMAGES GMBH/ALAMY

How To

Getting here & around La Ciénaga is the main trailhead, 30km west of Jarabacoa and reachable by *públicos* (shared taxis).

When to go Hiking is possible year-round, but the drier months (November to March) are the most popular.

What's in a name? Pico Duarte is named after Juan Pablo Duarte, one of the DR's founding fathers, of whom a statue sits on the summit. Before the dictator's death in 1961, it was called Pico Trujillo.

MAURITIUS IMAGES GMBH/ALAMY

The Climb

Rising from the heart of the Cordillera Central, which spans a third of the island, is **Pico Duarte** (3098m), the DR's highest mountain and the world's 79th by prominence. Making up part of the adjoining **Parque Nacional Armando Bermúdez** and **Parque Nacional José del Carmen Ramírez**, five routes lead to the summit, with treks taking anywhere from two to five days to complete.

La Ciénaga de Manabao Commonly known as La Ciénaga or Manabao, this is the most popular trailhead. This small settlement 30km west of Jarabacoa offers not only the most accessible starting point, but also the shortest and easiest route; hence, it is favored by most tour operators. From here, it's a 23km trek (one-way) to the summit, with 18km covered on the first day. The trail ascends

MAURITIUS IMAGES GMBH/ALAMY

Reaching the Top

Pico Duarte is not conquered; it is honored. The first day demands 18km of continuous ascent through living forest. After a night's rest, the final kilometers seal the achievement. At the summit, you discover you were always stronger than you believed.

Estela Ros, *Rancho Baiguate guide ranchobaiguate.com*

Left Parque Nacional Armando Bermúdez **Top left** Hikers at the summit of Pico Duarte **Above** Hikers in Parque Nacional Armando Bermúdez

2275m through pristine wilderness, crossing fern-filled valleys, pine forests and rivers, with abundant birdlife and ridgeline views. Hikers spend the night at **La Compartición campground** (2450m), enjoying dinner and a night under the stars. Day two is an early start with a 5km push to the summit timed for sunrise over the Cordillera Central. Most tours return to Compartición for a night before the descent.

Mata Grande The second-most popular trail is a tougher 45km trek with a 3800m vertical ascent that crosses Duarte's sister peak, **Pico La Pelona**. The other three routes – from Sabaneta, Las Lagunas and Constanza – are rarely used, more challenging and not offered by tour companies, meaning trekkers must arrange all logistics independently.

Organized Treks

Recommended operators departing from La Ciénaga include **Rancho Baiguate** (rancho baiguate.com), **Jaraventura** (jaraventura.

Lungs of a Nation

In the heart of the Central Highlands lie conjoined national parks: **Parque Nacional Armando Bermúdez** and **Parque Nacional José del Carmen Ramírez**. Together, they cover some 1500 sq km of verdant alpine mountains (including Pico Duarte), pristine valleys, old-growth forests and rivers. It's a region home to Hispaniola's richest biodiversity, with endemic species like the Hispaniolan parakeet, Hispaniolan parrot and black-throated blue warbler found only here. Established in the late 1950s, the parks were created to protect against the deforestation devastating Haiti's side of the Cordillera Central, safeguarding clean water sources that supply 90% of the DR's freshwater and a third of its electricity.

KAREL RASIN/SHUTTERSTOCK

Far left View over Parque Nacional Armando Bermúdez **Left** Hispaniolan parrot **Below** Cargo mules

com), **Pico Duarte Tours** (picoduartetours.com) and **Guias de Alturas** (guiasdealturas.com). For the Mata Grande route, **Camping Tours** (camping tours.net) is the most reliable.

Expect to pay between US$365 and US$550 per person for organized treks, which typically include meals, tents, sleeping bags, guides (check if they speak English), entrance fees, pack mules and (sometimes) even hot showers.

If you're keen to bag additional peaks like **La Pelona** (3084m) and **La Rusilla** (3038m), both Guias de Alturas and Pico Duarte Tours offer extended trips.

Going Solo

For those wanting to go solo, it's possible to arrange guides, mules and supplies directly in La Ciénaga, though it's best to bring your own tent, sleeping bag and gear. Note that hiring a guide is compulsory, and they'll require you to take at least one mule – essential for carrying water and other supplies.

Essential items to pack include warm and wet-weather clothing, sturdy hiking boots, spare shoes for camp, a flashlight, sunscreen, insect repellent and a dry bag to protect your gear. Don't forget energy bars and extra snacks for the trail.

FROM LEFT: MAURITIUS IMAGES GMBH/ALAMY; MAURITIUS IMAGES GMBH/ALAMY

28 Cultural SANTIAGO

MUSEUMS | MONUMENTS | MARKETS

The big smoke of the Central Highlands, Santiago (officially Santiago de los Caballeros) is the nation's second-largest city. Founded in 1495, it's one of the oldest European settlements in the Americas, so there's always going to be plenty to see here in terms of history, museums and culture – not forgetting cigars (p188), merengue (p186) and Carnival (p180).

MAURITIUS IMAGES GMBH/ALAMY

How To

Getting here and around Santiago's airport, 12km south of downtown, is served by major airlines. Taxis (US$20 one-way) and ride-hailing apps can get you into town. Caribe Tours buses connect Santiago to Puerto Plata (1¼ hours) and Santo Domingo (2½ hours).

When to go Year-round, but Carnival in February is certainly a highlight. As is the baseball.

All in the family Santiago was founded in 1495 by Bartholomé Columbus, Christopher's often-overlooked but equally adventurous brother.

SEA2SEA PHOTOGRAPHY/ALAMY

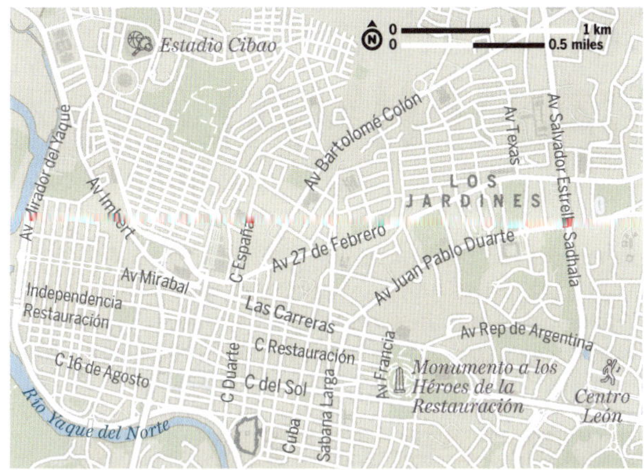

Museums Santiago's premier cultural attraction, **Centro León** (centroleon.org.do; adult/child RD$150/100; closed Mon), is one of the Dominican Republic's best museums. Housed in a striking postmodern building, this beloved institution – funded by the León Jimenes family's tobacco fortune – offers a rich showcase of Dominican art, culture and identity. Highlights include an outstanding collection of 20th-century modernist works, featuring celebrated artists like Yoryi Morel and Celeste Woss y Gil, whose *Autorretrato con Cigarrillo* (Self-Portrait with Cigarette) stands out as an iconic piece. Beyond the art, the museum has impressive galleries covering the island's biodiversity and anthropology that delve into the DR's cultural diversity, including standout displays on the indigenous Taínos. Its gift shop is a fantastic spot to pick up books on Dominican art and culture, as well as Taíno keepsakes. In the evenings, Centro León often hosts live merengue performances, art-house film screenings and other cultural events.

Monuments Another must-see is the **Monumento a los Héroes de la Restauración** (entry RD$100; closed Mon). In true dictator style, this imposing 67m marble structure, topped with an obelisk, was built by Rafael Trujillo in 1944 as a shrine to himself. After his death, it was rededicated to honor the soldiers who fought in the 1863–65 War of Restoration. Climb the 365 steps for panoramic views and visit the Dominican history exhibits.

Bottom left Centro León
Top left Monumento a los Héroes de la Restauración

The 'Valley of Death'

If baseball in the US is as American as apple pie, in the DR it's as Dominican as *La Bandera*, the beloved national dish. And there's no better place to catch a game than Santiago (November to February), home of the legendary **Águilas Cibaeñas** (aguilas.com.do). Known as the 'Valley of Death,' their home ground, **Estadio Cibao**, is the largest baseball stadium in the country, a fortress known for its passionate hometown fans. From March to August, it transforms to host soccer (football), serving as home ground for **Cibao FC** (cibaofc.com).

29 Celebrating CARNIVAL

COLOR | COSTUMES | PARTY

When is the best time to visit the Dominican Republic? There's only one answer: February for Carnival! Sure, prices and crowds rise, but the explosion of color, music and energy is unbeatable. And the Central Highlands is where you want to be: La Vega steals the show as the nation's most famous, while Santiago also hosts memorable celebrations.

CONSTANTIN MEEHAN/SHUTTERSTOCK

How To

Getting here and around La Vega is 38km southeast of Santiago and is linked by bus to Santo Domingo (1½ hours), Jarabacoa (one hour), Puerto Plata (two hours) and Sosúa (2½ hours).

When to go February is peak Carnival season, but events are also held in January and March.

Watch out for Diablo Cojuelo (Limping Devil), the main Carnival character who (playfully) whips people in the streets with a *vejiga* (inflated animal bladder).

VW PICS/GETTY IMAGES

Bottom left Swordsmen, La Vega Carnival parade **Top left** Carnival performer **Left** Display in the Museo del Carnaval Vegano

Viva La Vega Though the DR's third-largest city is usually a dusty, nondescript, industrious town, come February La Vega explodes with life as the country's Carnival hot spot. Every Sunday throughout February, around 900,000 revelers flood the streets for DR's biggest and wildest party, celebrated with flamboyant costumes and frightening Diablo Cojuelo masks. Expect high-spirited parades, concerts and raucous street parties to a nonstop soundtrack of merengue, samba and reggaeton.

Not only is La Vega's legendary Carnival the biggest, most colorful and boisterous in the DR, it's also the oldest in all the Americas – dating centuries before Rio de Janeiro even existed as a town, and more than 250 years before its now world-famous celebration began.

To learn more, visit the **Museo del Carnaval Vegano** (museocarnavalvegano.org.do) inside the restored 19th-century Don Zoilo Palace, with exhibits on costumes, history and traditions.

Santiago shindig Just 40 minutes away by bus, Santiago's Carnival may be tamer than La Vega's, but it's still one of the nation's very best. Celebrations stretch over four Sundays from February into early March at Parque Central. Santiago is famed for its stunning, intricate *caretas* (masks), honored each year with an international competition. Festivities peak in the neighborhoods of La Joya and Los Pepines.

Visit **Palacio Consistorial**, a museum within the former town hall (1895), displaying prize-winning masks and festival posters.

Like a Local

This is the Carnival that became a city. With roots dating to the 16th century, La Vega is home to one of the country's most important cultural celebrations. Held every February, it combines religious, historical and festive traditions and is notable for its colorful costumes, especially the 'devils with limping legs' – the event's main and emblematic figure. During Carnival, the streets are filled with music, *comparsas* (troupes), parades and joy. It is a space where creativity, local identity and community participation are strongly manifested. For the city of La Vega, the Carnival represents pride, tradition, and an important national tourist and cultural attraction.

Martiel Read, *Museo del Carnaval Vegano*

Carnival

FAMED, FUN-FILLED, CULTURAL FESTIVAL

Though not as internationally renowned as Rio de Janeiro, Carnival in the Dominican Republic is a major event. Celebrated nationwide every February, it bursts with vibrant color, sound and energy, uniting Dominicans of all ages in a joyous festival of music, tradition and cultural pride.

Left Musicians, Punta Cana Carnival **Center** Santiago Carnival **Right** Performers, Punta Cana Carnival

ALEKSANDR RYBALKO/SHUTTERSTOCK

The History

Carnival in the DR dates back to the mid-1500s, making it the OG of America's street parties. Originating with Spanish colonizers, it was initially tied to Catholic traditions, marking a time of indulgence before the austerity of Lent. Like most other Latin American Carnivals, the Dominican version has shifted away from religious observance, focusing more on the celebration itself, so today, it follows a fixed schedule throughout February, rather than aligning with Lent.

The festivities originally served as a protest, mocking the customs of the colonial elite. The costumes – cloaks, shiny shirts and jingle bell–embellished trousers – were a satire of Spanish medieval knights. Over time, Carnival evolved into something uniquely Dominican, blending Taíno, African and Spanish Catholic influences while incorporating plenty of humor to become the vibrant showcase it is today.

The Music

Carnival sees the streets fill with color, glitter and the extravagant costumes of performers parading to the vibrant soundtrack of traditional and modern Dominican music. Blaring from sound systems and live bands, merengue, *bachata*, reggaeton and *dembow* create a pulsating energy that's at the heart of these exuberant celebrations. Traditionally, merengue is regarded as DR's national music, and today its fast-paced rhythm and lively beat is the most prominent genre during Carnival, getting everyone on their feet. Dembow – a genre closely related to reggaeton – is in vogue with the new generation of Dominicans for its fast tempo, heavy bass and repetitive beats.

VICENTEGARRIDOJ/SHUTTERSTOCK

ORIOLE GIN/SHUTTERSTOCK

Iconic Characters

Dominican Carnival is known for its iconic characters, each representing different regions, towns or organizations. These masked *comparsa* (dance troupes) display their own unique costumes and traditions. Taking center stage is the Diablo Cojuelo, the mischievous 'Limping Devil,' Carnival's most famous figure. This character is easily recognized by its elaborate papier-mâché mask (which varies in grotesqueness depending on the city) and vibrant costume. The Diablo Cojuelo carries a *vejiga,* a balloon-like whip traditionally made from cow or pig bladders, though today it is usually made of rubber. This mischievous devil uses the *vejiga* to playfully smack passersby, especially women, who are traditionally often targeted.

> Over time, Carnival evolved into something uniquely Dominican, blending Taíno, African and Spanish Catholic influences while incorporating plenty of humor.

Other notable characters include Roba La Gallina, a man dressed as a woman, known as the 'chicken thief,' who is punished by having chicken feathers stuck to him and being forced to walk through the streets in public. Los Indios are figures representing the indigenous people of Hispaniola, adorned with feathers and body paint. Los Guloyas are descendants of the Afro-Caribbean community, recognized for their vibrant costumes and cultural significance. In 2005, UNESCO declared Los Guloyas a Masterpiece of the Oral and Intangible Heritage of Humanity.

Top Five Carnivals

La Vega

The original, biggest and best Carnival in the DR, with month-long festivities incorporating traditions dating back to 1520.

Santiago

Known for parades, concerts and the iconic Lechones – costumed guardians in pig masks and ruffled suits.

Santo Domingo

The capital's Malecón hosts the country's largest parade during the last weekend of February.

Punta Cana

Tourists and locals dance all night to merengue and Dominican rhythms at lively beachside celebrations.

Montecristi

Infamous for its intense 'Bulls and Civilians' event, where participants whip-crack one another. Best watched from afar!

Costumes of **CARNIVAL**

1 Diablo Cojuelo
Carnival's most iconic character wears a gruesome horned mask and whips crowds playfully with an inflated animal bladder.

2 Los Indios
A homage to the Taínos, they reenact scenes with bow and arrows while dressed in body paint, feathers, beads and sacks.

3 Los Ali Babas
Inspired by Ali Baba, these performers wear sequin-covered costumes and turbans, busting Arabian-inspired dance moves.

4 Los Africanos
These characters honor enslaved ancestors with painted black skin, palm-leaf skirts and vibrant dancing.

5 Califé
Traditional Dominican Carnival character in a tall hat and tuxedo who uses rhymes and satire to bring current social affairs to light.

6 Los Lechones de Santiago
Santiago's main character wears a horned mask (representing colonial greed) and playfully cracks rope whips as guardian of the Carnival.

7 Los Taimáscaros
The main character of Puerto Plata is a devil in a costume symbolizing DR's mix of cultural heritage including Taíno, African and Spanish influences.

8 Los Guloyas
Traditional troupe of Cocolo dancers dressed in bedazzling costumes representing migrants of this Afro-Caribbean community.

9 Roba La Gallina
The comical 'chicken thief' is a popular character in exaggerated drag, carrying a parasol and handbag containing a stolen chicken.

01 ORIOLE GIN/SHUTTERSTOCK, JOINTSTAR F/SHUTTERSTOCK, **02** YAKOV OSKANOV/SHUTTERSTOCK, **03** SANJUANERO88/WIKIMEDIA/CC BY-SA 4.0, **04** CARLOS NIN GOMEZ/SHUTTERSTOCK, **05** CARLOS NIN GOMEZ/SHUTTERSTOCK, **06** MARIO DE MOYA F/SHUTTERSTOCK, MADDYZ F/SHUTTERSTOCK, **07** ORIOLE GIN/SHUTTERSTOCK, JOINTSTAR F/SHUTTERSTOCK, **08** MARIO DE MOYA F/SHUTTERSTOCK, **09** MARIO DE MOYA F/SHUTTERSTOCK

30 Merengue in SANTIAGO

DANCING | MUSIC | CLUBS

Think partying in the Dominican Republic is only for Carnival? Think again. Santiago, the birthplace of rhythmic, infectious merengue, is known for keeping people on dance floors until the early hours. This city in the Central Highlands is the heart of merengue, where it all kicked off and continues to thrive.

MEDIANEWS GROUP/READING EAGLE/GETTY IMAGES

How To

Getting here and around Most of Santiago's clubs are downtown and near the historic center. Calle RC Tolentino has a lively strip of bars.

When to go Weekends are busy, so come early if you want to eat, but otherwise things don't get kicking until midnight.

Safety Though perfectly safe by day, after a night out clubbing in Santiago it's best to take an Uber or taxi.

JON MCLEAN/ALAMY

Rhythmic beat of the nation Merengue holds a special place in Dominican culture and identity. So much so, that not only is November 26 National Merengue Day, but in 2016, UNESCO recognized it as an Intangible Cultural Heritage of Humanity. Santo Domingo may be DR's hot spot for nightlife, but as the birthplace of *merengue típico* (the traditional form of merengue), Santiago remains a key player in the country's music scene. In a city that's produced many of the DR's most renowned merengue musicians, its ubiquitous rhythms blare from speakers on the street and in taxis, buses and bars. Though a new generation of musicians have infused contemporary styles like *dembow,* hip-hop and reggaeton into the mix, they've also helped revitalize *merengue típico,* bringing back a sound that had fallen out of favor with today's youth.

Merengue bars In Santiago, there are several venues where merengue thrives. **Casa Bader** (casabader.com), founded in 1939, offers traditional live music on weekends. **Centro León**, the city's premier museum and cultural center, hosts live performances every Saturday. **Barajando Bar** and **Ahí-Bar** are great spots for both merengue music and dancing, while the weekly block party on **Calle Cuba** in Los Pepines on Sundays provides a lively atmosphere. For those looking to learn the steps, **Academia de Baile Sabor Latino** (@saborlatinoacademy) offers dance lessons that immerse you in the rhythm of merengue.

Top left Couple dancing to merengue music **Bottom left** Merengue band

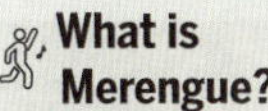

What is Merengue?

You're sitting there chatting and suddenly you hear a four-beat rhythm that makes your feet move without being able to stop them. You stand up and look around for someone to dance with, not caring if it's someone you know or not, but you hurry because you know that if you don't ask someone to dance, you'll be left with no one to dance with. Dancing, you forget about everything: your problems, what time it is or even who you're dancing with. You only hear the music playing in time with the swaying of waists from left to right. That's merengue!

Alex Rodriguez, *Academia de Baile, Santiago @saborlatinoacademy*

31 CIGAR Country

PRODUCTION | TOURS | FESTIVALS

Alongside beaches, merengue, baseball and rum, cigars are one of the iconic symbols of the DR. And it's here in the lush, tropical climate of the Cordillera Central where world-class tobacco is grown for some of the finest premium cigar brands. To witness the craftsmanship, visit Santiago's renowned cigar factories and experience the entire leaf-to-smoke process firsthand.

NURPHOTO/GETTY IMAGES

How To

Getting here and around Most of Santiago's factories are located 6km east in Tamboril, a famous cigar-making town. Take a passing *guagua*, from where it's a short walk. Otherwise take an Uber.

When to go February for the Procigar Festival.

Health warning Keep in mind that, as tobacco is addictive and carcinogenic, making (and smoking) cigars can be extremely harmful to people's health.

HEX1848/WIKIMEDIA/CC BY-SA 2.0

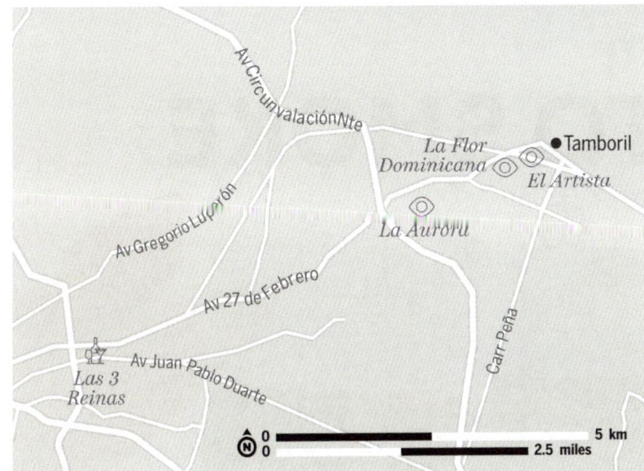

A storied history As the region where cigars were first produced in the Dominican Republic, taking a tour of a factory is a quintessential Santiago experience. It's only fitting to start at **La Aurora** (laaurora.com.do), the oldest and most renowned cigar maker. Established in 1903, guides take you through every step of the process: from seed germination and drying tobacco leaves to seeing both hand- and machine-rolled cigars being made. At the end, you'll receive complimentary cigars, and the gift shop, stocked with premium cigars and rums, will make any aficionado's eyes light up. Be sure to book in advance via email or phone.

Farms and tours Another top stop is **La Flor Dominicana** (laflordominicana.com) in Tamboril, the biggest manufacturer in the region since 1994, and known for its hand-rolled cigars. As tours aren't always available, calling ahead is recommended. For a more intimate experience, visit **El Artista** (elartista.com.do), a family-owned factory producing premium cigars since 1956. Tours are available by prior arrangement.

Lounging around If you're in town, don't miss **Las 3 Reinas** (The Three Queens), a classy female-owned cigar lounge with a walk-in humidor offering high-quality cigars, beers and rums in a relaxed setting.

Celebrate good times If you're lucky enough to visit during February's Carnival, you'll also have the chance to experience the **Procigar Festival** (procigar.org). This annual event includes factory and tobacco field tours, along with exclusive cigar tastings.

Bottom left La Aurora cigar factory **Top left** Worker rolls a cigar, La Flor Dominicana

Dominican vs Cuban Cigars

While Cuban cigars have long epitomized the gold standard in quality, Dominican cigars have steadily gained recognition for their hand-rolled craftsmanship and distinct character. After the Cuban Revolution, many master cigar makers relocated to the Dominican Republic, establishing it as one of the world's leading producers of premium cigars. Today, Cuban cigars remain more expensive and harder to access due to trade restrictions, while Dominican cigars offer greater availability, impressive consistency and a wide range of options.

Cigars from **SEED TO SMOKE**

01 Plant the seeds
Seeds are cultivated in greenhouses, where they are planted in trays to germinate and sprout for six weeks before being sown by hand in the soil outdoors.

02 Tobacco leaves
Fifty days later there is a fully grown tobacco plant, comprising three different-sized leathery leaves, each used for different components – from filler to wrapper.

03 Curing
After harvesting, they are taken to a barn to hang from the ceiling to dry for 60 days, turning them from vibrant green to dark brown.

04 Fermentation
Once dried, leaves are moved to the factory for fermentation – a meticulous, hands-on process involving constant rotation taking months to years.

05 Sorting
Leaves are sorted by purpose: from wrapper, binder and filler to size, shape and quality.

06 Aging
Leaves are then bundled in bales and placed in cedar bins to age for up to five years to mature the flavor.

07 Production
Master blenders prepare fillers using two to six leaves depending on the flavor profile. They pack the leaf evenly so it burns smoothly and cover it with the leaf binder before pressing it in a mold.

08 Rolling
Master cigar rollers select the best wrapper leaves and hand slice with a crescent-shaped blade.

09 Finishing
Workers trim and secure with a cap made of tobacco leaf to seal the cut end with vegetable paste. Once rolled, they're left to rest for at least six months.

10 Final product
Kick back and relax with the finished cigar, enjoyed even more now that you know what's gone into making it.

01 SKT STUDIO/SHUTTERSTOCK, **02** ALEKS KHAN/SHUTTERSTOCK, **03** AUTHORSIMAGE/ALAMY STOCK, **04** AUTHORSIMAGE/ALAMY, **05** SAMO TREBIZAN/SHUTTERSTOCK, **06** NURPHOTO/GETTY IMAGES, **07** NURPHOTO/GETTY IMAGES, **08** JON ARNOLD IMAGES LTD/ALAMY, **09** RJ LERICH/SHUTTERSTOCK, **10** CEPHAS PICTURE LIBRARY LTD/ALAMY

32 Cacao CITY

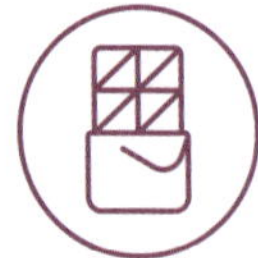

CACAO | TASTING | TOUR

Here's one you're going to love: a visit to a chocolate factory! Set in the lush Valle del Cibao near San Francisco de Macorís, here sweet tooths can indulge in the region's rich, unique flavors, all while learning about the fascinating process behind this organic industry.

SIMON RAWLES/ALAMY

How To

Getting here and around Located just outside San Francisco de Macorís, the chocolate factory is 1½ hours from Santiago or two hours from Santo Domingo.

When to go Year-round, though it's best to avoid the rainy months (April to October).

Did you know? Though introduced by Spanish colonizers in the 16th century, cacao here has developed a uniquely Dominican flavor thanks to its mixed genetic base and fermentation methods.

GAUTIER STEPHANE/ALAMY

Bottom left Sendero del Cacao
Top left Cacao bean harvest

Farm and factories As a top 10 global producer, cacao is one of the Dominican Republic's most important crops, of which 60% is grown in the Central Highlands. A short 15-minute drive from San Francisco de Macorís takes you to **Sendero del Cacao** (Cocoa Trail; cacaotour.com), where you'll explore an organic cacao plantation to learn every step of the process – from harvesting cacao pods to fermenting, drying, roasting, grinding, blending and molding. The sweetest part of the tour is, of course, the chocolate factory, where you'll sample hot chocolate made with onsite cacao, before taste-testing your way through the various stages and making your own chocolate bar. The gift shop offers traditional *bolas de cacao* (raw chocolate balls for making hot chocolate), as well as finely crafted chocolate bars of varying strengths. Comprehensive tours offer a deeper dive into the whole process. Other great organic cacao factories to visit include **Chocal** (chocalaltamira.wordpress.com), a female-owned collective empowering local women, and **Hacienda Cufa**. Both are about an hour north of Santiago.

Ecotourism experiences For a grassroots experience, get in touch with **Fundación Loma Quita Espuela** (facebook.com/FundLomaQuitaEspuela), which does a great job of protecting the **Reserva Cientifica Loma Quita Espuela** through its ecotourism initiatives. Enjoy guided hikes into the DR's largest rainforest to visit small cacao farms, swim in natural pools and visit Taíno caves. It also arranges treks to the top of Loma Quita Espuela (942m).

Organic Beans

The Dominican Republic is the world's largest exporter of certified organic cocoa, supplying 70% of global organic cocoa. Most of the country's cocoa comes from small-scale farmers in Fairtrade-certified co-ops such as **CONACADO** (conacado.com.do) and **COOPROAGRO** (cooproagro.org), which focus on sustainable agroforestry practices.

Through **Earthworm** (earthworm.org), the **Cacao Forest** (cacaoforest.org) launched its model in 2015 to promote shade-grown cacao under native and fruit trees, benefiting local farmers and preserving the environment, all while producing a better-quality product.

33 Smell the COFFEE

COFFEE | TOURS | MOUNTAINS

We've brought you cigars, chocolate and Carnival, and now it's time for one of life's other great pleasures: coffee! Here in the Cordillera Central mountain range, you'll find the country's most fertile soils, and around Jarabacoa, you'll find organic coffee plantations producing world-class beans. Take a bean-to-cup tour to see firsthand how your brew is cultivated, harvested and roasted.

MAURITIUS IMAGES GMBH/ALAMY

How To

Getting here and around Spirit Mountain is 24km southwest of Jarabacoa, accessed by 4WD along the highway to Manabao, from where you turn off a dirt road.

When to go Year-round, but the drier months (November to March) are more suitable for forest walks, as well as the harvesting season.

Shade-grown cultivation A sustainable technique of growing coffee takes place under the natural canopy of forest cover rather than clearing the land.

TODD AARON SANCHEZ/SHUTTERSTOCK

SA2UKEDR/SHUTTERSTOCK

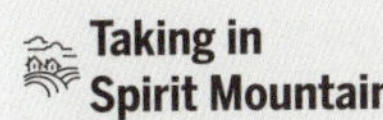

Bottom left Coffee plantation **Top left** Tour, Monte Alto Coffee Factory **Left** Coffee beans ripening

Sustainable farm tours A pilgrimage for coffee lovers is the trip up to **Spirit Mountain** (spiritmountaincoffee.com) to visit its sustainable, organic coffee plantation. Set at an elevation of 1200m on a 350-acre tract of tropical rainforest, the plantation practices ecofriendly agroforestry, growing coffee under the shade of trees. On guided tours (per person RD$1000), you'll learn how coffee is grown, harvested and roasted, before savoring a cup of its single-origin beans. The retreat also offers atmospheric solar-powered treehouse accommodations (double US$100, including breakfast), or enjoy the unpowered campsites, perfect for stargazing under the Dominican night skies. Guided walks, bird-watching, horseback riding and mountain biking are all also on the cards.

Factory tours For a different perspective on coffee production, visit the third-generation family-owned **Monte Alto Coffee Factory** (ramirezcoffee.com). Located just outside Jarabacoa, this larger-scale operation offers tours (RD$500, including a bag of coffee) that take you through the entire coffee-making process, offering insights into where your daily coffee comes from. While it's more easily accessible than Spirit Mountain, it lacks the rural experience, as tours don't include visits to the nearby coffee farm in Manabao, located 30 minutes outside town. Still, it's a great option for those looking to learn about coffee on a larger scale.

Taking in Spirit Mountain

At Spirit Mountain, you'll ride world-class mountain-biking trails, hike through kilometers of pristine forest and spot rare birds like the Hispaniolan trogon in one of the island's richest birding habitats. From the farm, take in sweeping views of Pico Duarte – the Caribbean's tallest peak. But the heart of Spirit Mountain is its coffee: cultivated under towering shade trees in a thriving highland rainforest. Here, visitors connect with nature, culture and sustainable farming in a way that's as unforgettable as the landscape itself. It's more than a destination – it's a living classroom in the wild beauty of the Dominican Republic.

Chad Wallace, *co-owner @spirit mountaincafe*

Listings

BEST OF THE REST

Salivating Santiago

Naturalis Té $

You may not have come all the way to the DR for food from Asia, but you'll be glad you did once you taste Naturalis Té's delicious and nutritious vegan and vegetarian dishes.

FrancePan $

Popular cafe-bakery serving croissants, coffee and other pastries that are perfect for a quick bite and break from sightseeing.

La Brasa $

A good spot for local dining is this open-air downtown barbecue joint on the western side of the Monument that lures in hungry punters for charcoal-grilled chicken.

La Campagna $

This popular cafe oozing homely charm has a tasty and healthy selection of sandwiches, salads and breakfast options. You'll find a few locations around the city.

El Tablon Latino $$

Looking out to the Monument, come by for modern takes on Latin American dishes with coconut mojitos, quality wines and delectable grilled meats – including a churrasco served with salsa chimichurri.

Il Pasticcio $$

Going strong since the 1990s, this is the place for authentic Italian cuisine – homemade pastas, seafood, meats, wine and tiramisu – paired with a bohemian atmosphere.

Camp David $$$

Make the journey up this 923m ridge (30 minutes northeast of Santiago) for the city's best fine dining, where you'll enjoy delicious traditional and contemporary Dominican cuisine.

Noah Restaurant & Lounge $$$

One of the city's finest for Dominican cuisine is this downtown restaurant at the Monument offering dishes such as charcoal-grilled octopus, goat cheese–stuffed empanadas, grilled meats and an unexpectedly long list of sushi.

Restaurant Pez Dorado $$$

Eclectic doesn't come close to describing the menu at this long-standing, high-end Santiago institution serving up Creole and Chinese dishes since the 1960s.

Saga Restaurant & Cigar Club $$$

It doesn't get more Dominican than fine dining and premium cigars. Don't worry, there's a separate non-smoking area so your steaks and seafood won't be ruined by the fumes.

Beer O'Clock in Santiago

Casa Bader

Going strong since 1939, here you'll find the biggest selection of beers in the city with

HACKENBERG-PHOTO-COLOGNE/ALAMY

Palacio Consistorial (p198)

200-plus varieties, along with tasty *quipes* (Dominican appetizers with ground beef) and live merengue.

Gallo Pelón Brew Pub

A must for craft-beer lovers is this popular brewhouse where you can sample an interesting range of ales and craft cocktails, paired with delicious artisanal pizzas and chicharron street tacos.

La Emergencia Jardín Cervecero

If you're dying for a beer, in case of emergency this place has you covered with its outdoor space perfect for a cold one and a great selection of craft ales, tapas and mains.

Pinta Beer Store

Downtown craft-beer bar with a wide selection of ales, matched with a beer-friendly menu of burgers, fries and pizzas.

Kicking on in Santiago

Barajando Bar

Right near the Monument, this happening spot has a good selection of drinks and live music that has folk busting moves on the dance floor.

Ahí-Bar

An open-air patio set above street level attracts people for casual drinks over dinner as a prelude to karaoke, DJs and live merengue. Especially busy on weekends after 10pm.

Kukara Macara Country Bar & Restaurant

Swing through the saloon doors and giddy up for some kitschy fun at this Wild West–themed bar at the Monument. Margaritas are served by cowboy and cowgirl waitstaff.

Atabeyra Bohemia

Cool divey place to enjoy craft beers, live bands and cultural events while puffing away on a cigar in the beer garden.

DIRK RENCKHOFF/ALAMY

Catedral de Santiago Apóstol

Puerta del Sol

Another option around the Monument, this relaxed bar has great city views, cold beers, good food and lively evenings with anything from karaoke, DJs and live music.

Tabu Room

If you're looking for a sweaty dance floor, heaving Tabu is one of your best bets for a night out, with DJs, good vibes and a lively crowd.

Around Santiago's Parque Duarte

Parque Duarte

In the city's center is a scenic, tree-filled square with monuments of DR's founding fathers and park benches on which to take a breather for some people-watching.

Catedral de Santiago Apóstol

On Parque Duarte's southern side is Santiago's main cathedral, which blends Gothic and neoclassical styles with impressive stained-glass windows. It contains the marble tomb of the late-19th-century dictator, Ulises Heureaux.

Palacio Consistorial

Santiago's former town hall sits on Parque Duarte's western side. It is now a small museum covering the city's history, including wonderful displays of Carnival masks.

Calle del Sol Indoor Market

This two-level shopping market is a maze of stalls selling souvenirs, cigars, paintings, jewelry and mamajuana (a spirit made with herbs, dried bark, rum, wine and honey).

Centro de la Cultura de Santiago

Half a block from Parque Duarte is this cultural center with a regular program of musical and theatrical performances. There's also a rotating exhibition of Dominican paintings in the small gallery.

Jarabacoa Bites & Imbibes

Café Colao $

This vibrant Instagrammable cafe specializes in single-origin Dominican coffee alongside tasty local dishes and breakfasts. It also offers accommodations and outdoor adventure tours.

El Fresco Bistro y Café $

A stylish, contemporary cafe with an enticing terrace on which to enjoy standout breakfasts, burgers, hearty salads, sandwiches and Dominican grilled mains paired with a choice of negronis and mai tais.

El Taino Restaurant & Pica Pollo $

If you're looking to eat local, this open-air *comedor* does flavorsome, cheap and cheerful Dominican dishes from breakfast through to dinner.

La Tinaja $

A solid choice for Dominican light bites such as *mofongos* and croquettes, as well as decent breakfasts, coffee and carrot cake. Not a bad stop all up.

La Baita $$

Set in a quaint log cabin in the hills and surrounded by greenery is this Italian restaurant north of town, popular for *fantastico* homemade pastas and wood-fired pizzas.

Parador Corazón de Jesús $$

Come for astonishing verdant mountain views at this open-air thatched cottage and dig into delicious wood-fired pork ribs or chicken (among other meats) accompanied by tasty Dominican sides.

Restaurant del Parque Galería $$

Overlooking Parque Central, this long-standing two-story restaurant with a wraparound balcony offers an extensive menu of Dominican dishes like *chivo* (goat) and churrasco, alongside the usual international offerings.

Jamaca de Dios Restaurant $$$

Enjoy international and Dominican dishes with sweeping views of Jarabacoa's lush countryside from the Caribbean's only rotating restaurant. Family-friendly by day, it transforms into a romantic, candlelit setting for dinner under the stars.

Balcón Restaurant & Lounge $$$

The jungle-covered hills near Salto de Baiguate are the last place you'd expect to find a Michelin-starred chef, yet Adin Langille heads up this upscale culinary retreat offering refined dishes with stunning mountain views.

DMITRY CHULOV/SHUTTERSTOCK

Santo Cerro

Venue Bar & Lounge

Jarabacoa gets pretty busy come weekends, when it's time to hit the clubs. This swanky lounge attracts well-dressed Dominicans looking to party.

Constanza Cuisine

Lorenzo's Restaurant $

On the town's west edge is this popular (especially on Sundays) lunch spot serving cheap and tasty Dominican mains, as well as sandwiches, pasta, pizza etc.

Mercado Municipal $

Set among the fertile soils of Cordillera Central, Constanza sits at the heart of the country's breadbasket, making this the go-to destination for the freshest produce in the DR.

Restaurant Aguas Blancas $$

This cozy cabin restaurant does Dominican staples and pastas, but its specialty is *guinea guisada* (guinea-fowl stew) and delicious house-made hot sauces. It gets chilly at night.

Sabores de Montaña $$

A great place to try delicious local specialties including *canastas de platano* (fried plantain cups filled with protein of your choice) washed down with cold beers and mojitos.

Beyond Carnival in La Vega

Museo Del Carnaval Vegano

As the birthplace of Carnival in the Americas, this is a great place to get the lowdown on the nation's famous festivities on a guided tour of this museum.

Santo Cerro

Legend says Columbus planted a cross here that defied destruction during a battle.

MAURITIUS IMAGES GMBH/ALAMY

Casa Museo Hermanas Mirabal

Today, come for valley views, the historic church and the Holy Hole said to mark the historic spot.

La Vega Vieja

After a 1562 earthquake, all that remains of the original site of La Vega are the Columbus-era ruins of a fort and church, plus a small museum of Spanish and Taíno relics.

Catedral de la Concepción

Overlooking the main plaza is La Vega's unusual cathedral featuring an unorthodox mix of Gothic and medieval fort style.

Passing Through Moca

Casa Museo Hermanas Mirabal

The former home of the Mirabal sisters, who were assassinated in 1960 for opposing dictator Trujillo's regime, is now a poignant museum preserved as they left it. Located 4km east of town in Salcedo.

Iglesia Corazón de Jesus

Moca's towering 110m-tall heritage-listed church features a panel of beautiful stained glass imported from Turin.

THE SOUTHWEST

NATURE | BEACHES | WILDLIFE

Explore **Lago Enriquillo**, the Caribbean's largest lake, home to iguanas and crocs (p211)

2hr from Barahona

Head to **San Cristóbal** for museums and ancient rock art (p222, p226)

1hr from Santo Domingo

Spot endemic birdlife at **Parque Nacional Sierra de Bahoruco** (p205)

1hr from Barahona

Boat out to **Bahía de las Águilas** for white-sand perfection (p205)

1hr from Playa Las Cuevas

Spot flamingos and iguanas at hyper-salinic **Laguna Oviedo** (p208)

2hr from Barahona

Constanza, Bonao, San Juan de la Maguana, San José de Ocoa, Presa de Jigüey-Aguacate, San Cristóbal, Presa de Valdesia, Neiba, Lago Enriquillo, Sierra de Martín García, Ázua, Laguna del Rincón, Barahona, Baní, Pedernales, Laguna de Oviedo, Península de Pedernales, Caribbean Sea

0 100 km
0 50 miles

THE SOUTHWEST
Trip Builder

Hidden away in the country's deep south lies some of the DR's most stunning natural scenery. Encompassing three interconnected national parks, this UNESCO Biosphere Reserve is the domain of iguanas, flamingos and crocodiles, and also the country's most pristine beach with its whitest, softest sands.

FROM LEFT: ULLSTEIN BILD /GETTY IMAGES, ALEXTIPTOP/SHUTTERSTOCK
PREVIOUS SPREAD: RUNECA/SHUTTERSTOCK

Practicalities

ARRIVING

Buses depart **Aeropuerto Internacional Las Américas** for San Cristóbal (one hour) and Barahona (three hours). **Sinchomiba**, Barahona's bus terminal, has *guaguas* (local buses) to Pedernales (two hours).

FIND YOUR WAY

Most main roads are well signed, but for national parks and rural areas, a GPS is highly recommended.

MONEY

Withdraw enough cash in bigger towns; ATMs are scarce from Barahona to Pedernales.

WHERE TO STAY

Place	Pros/Cons
Playa Las Cuevas	Beach-side base with glamping; perfect launching point for Bahía de las Águilas.
Parque Nacional Sierra de Bahoruco	Villa Barrancoli, run by a bird tour operator, is perfect for twitchers. No accommodations in the park itself.
Barahona	Convenient base for national parks. Not a destination in itself.
San Cristóbal	Beaches and plenty of attractions close by.

GETTING AROUND

Bus Caribe Tours has regular services to Barahona and San Juan de la Maguana. (caribetours.com.do)

Car Best arranged in Santo Domingo. Strongly consider getting a 4WD.

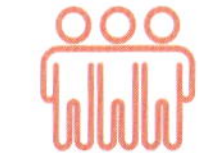

Tours The most convenient way of visiting many of the southwest's major attractions.

TOP: LOVEMYDESIGNS/SHUTTERSTOCK
BOTTOM: TOYAKISPHOTO/SHUTTERSTOCK

EATING & DRINKING

You can expect an array of delicious grilled fish and seafood, cold beachside beers, piña coladas and fresh coconuts. In larger towns you'll find restaurants offering both Dominican and international cuisine, particularly Italian and Mexican. *Comedores* dish up local staples of grilled meats, fish, conch, *pica pollo* (fried chicken; picture bottom) and *tostones* (fried plantain).

Best Mexican
Rincón Mexicano (p230)

Must-try *mofongos*
Rancho Tipico (p228)

JAN–MAR
Best for flamingos and wildlife at Laguna Oviedo.

MAR–JUN
Blooming cactus flowers in Lago Enriquillo.

JUN–AUG
Sea turtles lay and hatch their eggs on beaches.

DEC–FEB
Sunny skies and fiestas make this the busiest time.

34 Escape to PARADISE

BEACH | BOATS | ISLANDS

The DR's far southwest is the stuff Caribbean dreams are made of: empty, pristine, white sandy beaches; warm gin-clear waters; and remote desert islands. With not a resort in sight, it's blissfully protected as part of Parque Nacional Jaragua, a UNESCO Biosphere Reserve.

VANZETTY DURANT/SHUTTERSTOCK

How To

Getting there Remote and hard to reach, there are two ways to get to Las Águilas: via a spectacular boat ride organized from Playa Las Cuevas or by 4WD navigating the dirt roads.

When to go Dry season (November to March) has the best beach weather. Aim for week-days when there are fewer day-trippers.

Did you know? Isla Alto Velo was briefly claimed by the US in 1856 under the Guano Islands Act.

FOTOREQUEST/SHUTTERSTOCK

The Bay of Eagles

Considered by many to be the most beautiful beach in the Dominican Republic, **Playa Bahía de las Aguilas** (Bay of Eagles Beach) could be that picture-perfect slice of paradise you've always dreamed of. Protected by the **Parque Nacional Jaragua**, this 8km remote stretch of white, powdery sand and crystal-clear turquoise waters has no restaurant and no hotels; instead, it's frequented only by day-trippers and diving brown pelicans.

Most visitors arrive by arranging a boat trip from Playa Las Cuevas, a scenic journey that passes dramatic cliff formations and is very much an adventure in itself. Ecofriendly operators include **Eco del Mar** (ecodelmar.com.do) and **Rancho Típico** (cuevadelasaguilas.com), which organize boat rides before returning to Playa Las Cuevas for beachside

JIMMYVILLALTA/GETTY IMAGES

Parque Nacional Jaragua

Bahía de las Águilas and its outlying islands are protected by the country's largest national park: the 1543-sq-km **Parque Nacional Jaragua**, which takes in marine, lake and terrestrial habitats. Jaragua is part of the larger UNESCO-listed Jaragua–Bahoruco–Enriquillo Biosphere Reserve, which spans the southwest DR.

Bottom left Boats moored in Bahía de las Águilas **Top left** Beach, Bahía de las Águilas **Above** Brown pelican

glamping and fresh seafood feasts. Otherwise, **Grupo Jaragua** (grupojaragua.org.do) is a recommended operator that uses expert local guides. Tours include snorkeling gear for exploring the nearby coral reefs. The area is a breeding ground for hawksbill and leatherback turtles, so inquire about those tours, too.

Island-Hopping

The other major draw to this remote, captivating southwest corner is its offshore islands – Beata and Alto Velo – both part of the Parque Nacional Jaragua. A paradise for nature lovers and adventurers, together they form an underwater mountain range that extends to the mainland and is accessible only by boat tour: Eco del Mar, Rancho Típico and **Ecotour Barahona** (ecotourbarahona.com) are all recommended operators.

The closer and more visited of the two islands is **Isla Beata**, which is no more than a cluster of rustic fishing shacks and coconut

The Beauty of Beata

Dare to explore new horizons, and I'd be happy to accompany you on this unique adventure to Isla Beata. Covering 42 sq km, it's the DR's second-largest island and part of the pristine Parque Nacional Jaragua. Beata's rich biodiversity includes endemic land species such as rhinoceros iguana, while its crystal-clear waters shelter diverse marine life, including corals and sea turtles. Once inhabited by the Taíno people of the Jaragua Chiefdom, the island still holds the rock art of these ancient inhabitants. Scenic hikes take in hidden unspoiled beaches, breathtaking views and dolphin sightings.

Pablo Feliz, *guide with AGUINAOVI grupojaragua.org.do, Whatsapp +1-829-889-758*

Left Isla Beata **Below** Parque Nacional Jaragua (p205)

palm–fringed beaches. (It's also a Dominican Navy outpost.) The island's most famous residents are rhinoceros iguanas, a rare species you'll see ambling along its beaches and fishing shacks. The island has a darker side too, and once housed a prison for political dissidents during Rafael Trujillo's dictatorship in the 1950s. Today, visitors can explore the haunting ruins of the prison's towers and buildings.

Further south lies the uninhabited islet of **Alto Velo**, the DR's southernmost point and (not surprisingly) one of its least-visited places. There are no beaches here so it's one for those who like rugged, wild, remote places. For panoramic views, scramble up to its highest point (250m) to reach the ruins of an old lighthouse; a two-hour (5km) return trek.

A sanctuary for birdlife, including the Caribbean's largest colony of sooty terns, the island is also home to endemic species found nowhere else, including the critically endangered Alto Velo curlytail and anole lizards. Consequently, it's part of a major restoration project under the **Island-Ocean Connection Challenge** (IOCC; jointheiocc.org) to restore vegetation destroyed from historical guano mining and eradicate introduced animals such as rats and feral cats.

FROM LEFT: JOEL LEGER/SHUTTERSTOCK, VW PICS/GETTY IMAGES

35 Salty Laguna OVIEDO

FLAMINGOS | IGUANAS | MUD BATHS

Striking saltwater Laguna Oviedo, a gorgeous green-hued lagoon in the Parque Nacional Jaragua's east, is famed for its rich biodiversity, and is home to flamingos and iguanas among other endemic species. Comprising a unique ecosystem, the lagoon is separated from the sea by an 800m sandbar, with seawater entering through underground karstic channels.

DANITA DELIMONT/ALAMY

How To

Getting there Laguna Oviedo is 3km north of Oviedo town, clearly marked off the coastal highway. Buses from Oviedo and Pedernales stop nearby; the last bus to Barahona leaves around 4pm.

When to go You'll see flamingos year-round, but winter (December to March) has the greatest numbers. Turtles can be sighted from April to August.

Pink power Naturally white, flamingos and spoonbills' rose-colored plumage comes from their diet of algae rich in carotenoid pigments.

MICHAEL DWYER/ALAMY

VW PIC/GETTY IMAGES

Bottom left Rhinoceros iguana **Top left** Flamingos **Left** Roseate spoonbills

Few sights evoke a more iconic Caribbean image than a flock of vivid pink flamingos wading gracefully through a serene, sunlit lagoon. It's this magical scene that awaits you at the hypersalinic **Laguna Oviedo**, where these flamboyant birds gather in its algae-rich waters.

Twitching While some flamingos do live here year-round, they are a migratory species, so it's best to check with **Grupo Jaragua** (grupojaragua.org.do) if they're around prior to your visit. Not to worry, though, as there are 150 other species for twitchers to tick off. Highlights include equally cool roseate spoonbills, endangered West Indian whistling ducks, red dish egrets, brown pelicans, herons, ibis, sandpipers and others.

Boat tours The lagoon contains 24 small islands, best explored via boat tour. These excursions offer close encounters with the rhinoceros iguana, an endemic, dinosaur-like species, and the chance to take a natural mineral-rich **mud bath**, famed for its skin-rejuvenating properties. From April to August, visitors may also spot leatherback turtles nesting, although sightings are far from guaranteed.

Bookings Head to the **visitor center** to pay the RD$150 park entrance fee and book tours, such as a 30-minute flamingo walking tour (RD$2500), one- or two-hour boat tour (RD$3500/4500) or turtle tour (RD$7000). Other excursions, such as visiting Bahía de las Águilas (RD$2000) and Taíno petroglyphs (RD$4000), are also available. Prices listed are per group.

Biodiversity Pioneers

Established in 1987, **Grupo Jaragua** (grupojaragua.org.do) is a local NGO set up to promote the sustainable management of biodiversity in Laguna Oviedo and the broader Jaragua–Bahoruco–Enriquillo Biosphere Reserve. Working closely with local communities, it promotes conservation and ecotourism, all while supporting livelihoods through guide training and employment. Though it doesn't offer tours directly, its informative website lists all available excursions run by the Oviedo Lagoon Guides Association (AGUINAOVI), complete with WhatsApp contact details for each certified guide.

36 Jurassic PARK

CROCODILES | BIRD-WATCHING | LAKE

Another piece of the Jaragua–Bahoruco–Enriquillo Biosphere Reserve puzzle is Parque Nacional Lago Enriquillo & Isla Cabritos. Home to the Caribbean's largest lake, the 200-sq-km Enriquillo is twice as salty as the sea and is home to American crocodiles, iguanas, pink flamingos and flowering cacti – making this a particularly photogenic destination.

SOTO.CREATIVO/SHUTTERSTOCK

How To

Getting there *Guaguas* run from Barahona to Neiba, where you change for La Descubierta (one hour). Tell the driver to drop you at the visitor center.

When to go March to June has blooming cactus flowers; December through April has flamingos. Avoid June to August when temperatures reach 50°C (122°F)!

Land of contrasts The DR is home to both the highest point in the Caribbean (Pico Duarte; 3098m) and also the lowest: Lago Enriquillo at 46m below sea level.

ULLSTEIN BILD/GETTY IMAGES

Iguanas Dinosaurs may have become extinct 65 million years ago, but at **Lago Enriquillo** you'd be forgiven for thinking otherwise. Here you'll come face-to-face with two very prehistoric-looking beasts: the rare **Ricord's iguana**, with its spiky back, and the massive 10kg **rhinoceros iguana**; both are endemic endangered species. Though they're seen around the visitor center (do not feed them!), to see them in their natural habitat head to **Isla Cabritos**, a small island in the lake formed from an ancient seabed.

Crocodiles While the temperatures here sizzle as high as 50°C, don't expect any cool, refreshing swims in Lago Enriquillo. It's home to some 200 hundred American crocodiles, one of the world's largest species, a fearsome-looking creature that can grow up to 7m in length. To see them, take an early morning boat tour. You can arrange boat operators and guides at the **visitor center** at the park's entrance.

Bird-watching But it's birds – not reptiles – that are the dinosaurs' closest relatives, and this park is teeming with them. Like nearby Laguna Oviedo, flamingos are the stars of the show from December to April, though in recent years numbers have declined. Still, with over 130 bird species recorded, including herons, ibises and egrets, bird-watchers will find plenty to keep them busy, especially near the Río de la Descubierta.

Bottom left Excursion boat, Isla Cabritos **Top left** Lago Enriquillo

Enriquillo, Taíno Warrior

Born along the shores of the lake that now bears his name, Enriquillo (1498–1535) was a Taíno *cacique* (chief) who led a historic resistance against Spanish colonizers. Today he's celebrated as a national hero who fought for indigenous rights and liberated both Taíno and African slaves from exploitation.

Near the lake, you'll find **Las Caritas** (The Faces) – pre-Taíno petroglyphs etched into a cliffside, which resemble the world's oldest smiley face. Though little is known about the site, legend holds that Enriquillo used it as a rebel base. Climb the rocks for a close-up view and stunning panoramas over the lake.

Wild Wonders of the Southwest

RARE AND INTRIGUING WILDLIFE

Rich in biodiversity, the Península de Pedernales is home to rare wildlife and bird species found nowhere else on the planet. It forms a key part of the country's first UNESCO Biosphere Reserve, spanning coastlines, cloud forests, lakes and mountains across three national parks.

Left American crocodile **Center** Hispaniolan emerald hummingbird **Right** Loggerhead turtle

ULLSTEIN BILD/GETTY IMAGES

Reptiles

Of all the fascinating reptiles you'll encounter in the DR's southwest, iguanas are the highlight. Endemic to Hispaniola, the impressive, giant, scaly rhinoceros iguana is a common sight in conservation areas such as Lago Enriquillo (p210), Laguna Oviedo (p208) and Isla Beata (p206). While they may appear menacing, they are generally docile; however, they are wild animals, so never feed them. Another critically endangered endemic species is the Ricord's iguana. Slightly smaller than the rhinoceros iguana, there's only 3000 of these beauties on the planet, so consider it a privilege to see them at Lago Enriquillo.

Other endemic lizards include the Alto Velo curlytail, Alto Velo anole and the tiny Jaragua gecko, which was discovered in 2001 and is believed to be the world's smallest reptile. These are all found only on Alto Velo (p207).

In stark contrast to these tiny creatures are the American crocodiles that inhabit the salty waters of Lago Enriquillo. One of the largest crocodile species in the world, they average 3m to 4m in length but can grow up to 7m.

There are no venomous snakes in the region, but the southwest is home to endemic species such as the Barahona red-headed racer and the Hispaniolan vine boa, first documented in 2020.

Birds

Parque Nacional Sierra de Bahoruco (p216) boasts 28 of Hispaniola's 32 endemic bird species, including the Hispaniolan trogon, emerald hummingbird, narrow-billed tody, western chat-tanager and Hispaniolan parrot.

NEIL BOWMAN/SHUTTERSTOCK

SAMI SARKIS/GETTY IMAGES

In Parque Nacional Jaragua (p209), bird-watchers can observe some 137 species, including 10 endemics and 47 migratory birds. This park also hosts the country's largest population of white-crowned pigeons and threatened ashy doves. Alto Velo island is home to the largest nesting colony of sooty terns in the Caribbean. However, the most sought-after bird by casual visitors is the Caribbean flamingo. Your best chance to see one is during winter at Laguna Oviedo and Lago Enriquillo. Other crowd favorites include the algae-pink stained roseate spoonbill and diving brown pelican.

The most sought-after bird by casual visitors is the Caribbean flamingo. Your best chance to see one is during winter at Laguna Oviedo.

Turtles

The southwest's warm coastal waters are home to four sea turtle species: green, leatherback, hawksbill and loggerhead. If you're lucky, you may encounter them while snorkeling, but you're more likely to see them nesting on the beach from May to October at Parque Nacional Jaragua's Bahía de las Águilas or Laguna Oviedo.

Mammals

Mammals are the least visible of the southwest's wildlife. The DR hosts only two endemic land mammals: the Hispaniolan hutia, a tree-climbing rodent, and the solenodon, a burrowing nocturnal insectivore. Both are endangered and extremely elusive.

Bird Resources

Ruta Barrancolí: A Bird-finding Guide to the Dominican Republic (2012) By Stephen Latta and Kate Wallace, featuring 33 maps and descriptions of 44 sites.

Birds of the West Indies By Herbert Raffaele et al, covers birds across the West Indies, including migratory species you may see in the DR.

ebird.org Drill down for hot-spot maps with recent and past sightings across the DR and worldwide. Invaluable.

caribbeanbirdingtrail.org Detailed sightings from across the DR's southwest and beyond. Great resource for local guides and tour operators, too.

birdscaribbean.org Features profiles on endemic and migratory birds across the Caribbean.

WILDLIFE
Watching

01 Rhinoceros iguana
Cyclura cornuta, an iconic species endemic to the southwest, grows up to 2m long.

02 Ricord's iguana
Cyclura ricordi, spiky backed reptiles seen around Lago Enriquillo.

03 Jaragua gecko
At 16mm in size, *Sphaerodactylus ariasae* stakes its claim as the world's smallest lizard – and vertebrae for that matter.

04 Caribbean flamingo
With it vibrant pink feathers, spindly legs and flexible neck, the world-famous *Phoenicopterus ruber* is a favorite; best spotted in Laguna Oviedo.

05 American crocodile
Weighing up to 900kg and growing up to 7m long, *Crocodylus acutus* is one of the world's largest crocodiles, with a thriving population in Lago Enriquillo.

06 Leatherback turtle
Hike through forest from Laguna Oviedo to see *Dermochelys coriacea*, the world's largest turtles, nesting in April and May.

07 Hispaniolan solenodon
One of two endemic mammal species in the DR, *Solenodon paradoxus* is a nocturnal shrew-like creature found in Parque Nacional Sierra de Bahoruco.

08 Roseate spoonbill
Spot pink-plumed *Platalea ajaja* wading in Laguna Oviedo, hoovering up fish, insects and crustaceans with spoon-shaped bills.

09 Hispaniolan parrot
The beautiful bright-green *Amazona ventralis* is endemic to Hispaniola and can be spotted in Parque Nacional Sierra de Bahoruco.

01 ERIC ISSELEE/SHUTTERSTOCK, **02** ROSTASEDLACEK/SHUTTERSTOCK, **03** M.R.BOBADILLA/WIKIMEDIA/CC BY-SA 4.0, **04** PUTTACHAT KUMKRONG/SHUTTERSTOCK, **05** PUTTACHAT MARTIN MECNAROWSKI/SHUTTERSTOCK, **06** MOLLY ALTSCHWAGER/SHUTTERSTOCK, **07** MARVIN DEL CID/GETTY IMAGES, **08** ERIC ISSELEE/SHUTTERSTOCK, **09** DEA / V GIANNELLA/GETTY IMAGES

Biodiversity HOT SPOT

BIRD-WATCHING | GORGE | HIKING

Now it's time for the lush, mountainous part of this UNESCO Biosphere Reserve – Parque Nacional Sierra de Bahoruco. Spanning 800 sq km, its varied landscapes stretch from desert lowlands to misty cloud forests, offering a rich biodiversity that's ideal for bird-watching and trekking.

MICHAEL DWYER/ALAMY

How To

Getting there and around Many visit as part of a tour (recommended). Otherwise, you'll need a 4WD, which is best hired from Santo Domingo and accessed from the town of Puerto Escondido – reached from the turnoff at Duvergé.

When to go Dry season from November to April is the best time for trekking.

Top tips In the mountains the average temperature is 18°C (64°F), and annual rainfall is between 1000mm and 2500mm – so bring wet, all-weather gear.

Bird-Watching

Don't forget your binoculars, as this is one of Dominican Republic's finest national parks for birdlife. Over 80 species inhabit the park, including 28 of Hispaniola's 32 endemics, which are found across a range of ecozones, from expansive, cool-climate valleys to mountain peaks draped in pine and cloud forests.

In the higher mountain habitat, keep an eye out for the emerald hummingbird, La Selle thrush, Hispaniolan spindalis, white-winged warbler, western chat-tanager and Hispaniolan parrot. At lower elevations you may see white-necked crows, flat-billed vireos and elusive bay-breasted cuckoos.

Highly recommended **Tody Tours** (todytours.com) was set up by ex-Peace Corps volunteer Kate Wallace (p218), who's been

PRISMA BY DUKAS PRESSEAGENTUR GMBH/ALAMY

Bottom left Parque Nacional Sierra de Bahoruco vista **Top left** View over Hoyo de Pelempito (p219)

guiding since 1997 and is an expert in the field. It operates out of rustic forest camp **Villa Barrancolí** (villabarrancoli.com; cabins per person US$75, camping with/without tents US$30/15), purpose-built for bird-watchers at 400m above the Lago Enriquillo basin – the perfect base camp for park excursions. With advance notice you can arrange meals and picnic provisions, even if you're not staying here, It collaborates with **Cua Birding** (cuabirding.com), led by passionate guide and photographer Iván Mota, who runs tailored bird-watching tours lasting one to 10 days.

Also inquire about trips into the surrounding cloud forest, where the habitat around Cachóte makes up a unique part of Bahoruco's ecosystem. Here trails reach altitudes of 1300m, passing through misty forest, mountains and remote communities with coffee plantations, all while offering scenic views and

Bird-watching with an Expert

The Sierra de Bahoruco offers a wonderful variety of habitats and associated plants and animals. I first came here with ornithologists for the excitement of spotting endemic bird species, those found only here in the world. Zapoten, the beginning of the cloud-forest zone, is where you must be at first light to see the rarest of the rare! I can get you there by leaving Villa Barrancolí at 4am with a local driver experienced to meet the challenge of one of the worst roads in the world (I have witnesses...). Come visit me!

Kate Wallace, *owner Tody Tours (todytours.com) and Villa Barrancolí (villabarrancoli.com)*

Flora of Bahoruco

From dry forests to cloud-covered peaks, Parque Nacional Sierra de Bahoruco is a biodiversity hot spot, home to some 1400 plant species. Of these, 439 are endemic. The park also hosts 166 orchid species – more than half of the nation's total, 32% of which are found nowhere else.

excellent bird-watching. At its western edge, **Loma del Toro** (2367m) is surrounded by pine forest savanna and offers sweeping views and rarer high-altitude bird species.

Putting the Gorge into Gorgeous

A highlight for many visitors to the Sierra de Bahoruco is the viewpoint overlooking **Hoyo de Pelempito** (Pelempito's Hole). Sitting in the park's southern zone, this monumental gorge is 2.5km wide, 7km long and plunges a stunning 700m. Enclosed by lush forest, you can gaze out over this crater-like geological depression (essentially a sinkhole) from the visitor center that sits perched at the edge of a forested cliff (1450m), offering far-reaching views of untouched national park taking in eight different climate zones. It has information (in Spanish) on the area's flora and fauna, and a number of short nature walks, with signs identifying the various plants.

To get here, you'll need a 4WD or to come on a tour; the turnoff is about 12km east of Pedernales, and leads you 13.5km to a ranger station (RD$100 entry), where the paved road continues for 16km before becoming a bumpy dirt track for the last 7km.

Left Broad-billed tody **Top** Trees in Parque Nacional Sierra de Bahoruco **Above** Hispaniolan trogon

38 Unearthing a TREASURE

RARE | BEAUTIFUL | BLUE

For a genuine 'only in the DR' experience, journey through the rainforest of northeast Península de Pedernales to reach the Larimar mines. This brilliant blue stone, found nowhere else on the planet, has only been mined since the 1970s. Today, the mines remain locally owned, and a museum offers visitors an authentic, grassroots glimpse into this local industry.

MARINA KRYUCHINA/SHUTTERSTOCK

How To

Getting there Unless you've hired a 4WD, this is one best visited on an organized tour. The mines are located 25km southwest from Barahona, accessed inland from the turnoff at El Arroyo. Check they're open before setting out.

When to go Aim for the dry season (November to April).

Did you know? Larimar is the DR's official stone. It has its own holiday, which is celebrated on November 22.

MELAMARI/SHUTTERSTOCK

Bottom left Larimar bracelets **Top left** Larimar stone **Left** Jewelry display, Escuela Taller y Museo Larimar

A true gem Matching the magnificence of the Caribbean's electric blue waters is this fetching turquoise gemstone formed from silicon-rich pectolite minerals. Larimar is found only in this neck of the woods across 1 sq km – a mere blip on Earth – and a trip into the rugged, remote mountainous region of Bahoruco to see the source of this gorgeous stone is a popular excursion for day-trippers. Don't expect BHP or Rio Tinto out this way; the ramshackle mines are very much locally run affairs with a shantytown feel. In the past, tours took you down the shafts, but at the time of research, the mines had been closed by government restrictions enforced to prevent over-extraction of the stone and for environmental sustainability reasons.

Tours Check ahead for the latest with **Ecotour Barahona** (ecotourbarahona.com) and **Larimar Eco Tours** (larimarecotour.com), both reliable choices for all-inclusive day tours running from Barahona.

Learn more In the meantime, **Escuela Taller y Museo Larimar** (Larimar School and Museum) provides a good background on the stone and has a workshop where you can meet the miners and buy jewelry. Prized for both its beauty and rarity, the highest-quality stones are a pure blue, turquoise color.

The Story of Larimar

A source of national pride, Larimar is one of the Dominican Republic's most beloved natural treasures – a rare, sky-blue gemstone found nowhere else on Earth. Not to be confused with blue amber, the DR's other famous semi-precious stone, Larimar was formed from volcanic activity and mineral-rich hydrothermal flows. Though first documented in 1916, it wasn't widely recognized until 1974, when Miguel Méndez and Peace Corps volunteer Norman Rilling rediscovered it near the Bahoruco Mountains. Méndez named the stone after his daughter, Larissa, and 'mar,' the Spanish word for sea, inspired by the turquoise hues of the Caribbean Sea.

39 Dictator DIGS

HISTORY | MUSEUMS | ARCHITECTURE

One for those into dark tourism is San Cristóbal, birthplace of dictator Rafael Trujillo, where you'll find a stark glimpse into his regime's excesses. In 1939, he renamed the province 'Trujillo,' a name later abandoned after his death. He filled the city with self-glorifying monuments and grand buildings, including two palatial residences – one of which he infamously never lived in.

Hato Damas
Río Jaina
Casa Caoba
San Cristóbal
Castillo del Cerro
Nigua
Boca de Nigua
0 5 km
0 2.5 miles

How To

Getting there Located 30km west of the capital, it's a one-hour bus trip from Santo Domingo. A bus to Barahona takes 3½ hours.

When to go Year-round

Did you know? As a reminder of Trujillo's regime, an empty pedestal stands across from the cathedral; it used to support a statue of Trujillo on horseback, but residents pulled it down after his death.

Castillo del Cerro Of the two lavish palaces Trujillo built in San Cristóbal, Castillo del Cerro is the most outrageous. It was built in 1947 for himself and his family at a staggering cost of US$3 million, yet they didn't spend a single night there because Trujillo didn't like it!

Perched on a hill, its name, 'Castle on the Hill,' fits the location but not the architecture: it's more mid-century Miami than medieval fortress, resembling a curved glass-and-concrete office block or the stern of a ship. Today, it houses the National Penitentiary School, a training center

Right Interior room, Castillo del Cerro

ALBUM/ALAMY

for future prison guards, adding to its intimidating feel. Guided weekday tours take you through lavish dining rooms and ballrooms, bedrooms with ornate ceilings and bathrooms decorated in colorful mosaic tiles. A small museum displays Dominican prison history, torture devices and a replica electric chair.

Casa Caoba If Trujillo didn't like his Castillo del Cerro, luckily for him he had another hilltop mansion to fall back on – as one does. Just above town, Casa Caoba was his mountain retreat, built in 1938 entirely from mahogany. It's been abandoned since his death and now lies in ruin with crumbling graffiti-splattered walls. Despite repeated promises to restore it, nothing has been done and it's been reclaimed by the surrounding forest and left to decay. The building's deterioration makes it unsafe to visit without a guide.

Trujillo's Dictatorship

In 1930, Rafael Trujillo seized power in the Dominican Republic following a rigged election, ruling with terror until his assassination in 1961. Known as 'El Jefe' (The Boss), he established a brutal dictatorship using death squads, racism and propaganda to suppress dissent. Trujillo is infamously remembered for the 1937 massacre of up to 35,000 Haitians, all while amassing vast wealth siphoned through state monopolies. In true cult-of-personality fashion, he renamed both the capital and the country's highest mountain after himself. Despite his atrocities, some Dominicans nostalgically recall his regime for its economic development.

40 Prehistoric GALLERIES

HISTORY | INDIGENOUS | PETROGLYPHS

Just 10km north of San Cristóbal lies Reserva Antropológica Cuevas del Pomier, one of the largest examples of prehistoric art discovered in the Caribbean. Spread across 57 limestone caves, the highlights are the five caves containing over 600 paintings – works created by the indigenous Igneri, Caribs and Taínos dating back over 2000 years.

JON G FULLER/VWPICS/ALAMY

How To

Getting there Located 10km north of San Cristóbal, you can take a taxi or *motoconcho* (motorcycle taxi). Guides can be arranged on arrival, but they don't always speak English, so visiting on an organized tour isn't a bad idea.

When to go Year-round

Did you know? There are actually three major sets of caves, but El Pomier is the only one open to the public.

JON G FULLER/VWPICS/ALAMY

JON G FULLER/VWPICS/ALAMY

Bottom left Entrance to Reserva Antropológica Cuevas del Pomier
Top left Interior, Cuevas del Pomier
Left Pictographs, Cuevas del Pomier

Under-the-radar artworks Despite protecting the most extensive collection of cave pictographs in the Caribbean, the **Reserva Antropológica Cuevas del Pomier** somehow remains under the radar. Located just outside San Cristóbal, it features 57 limestone caves, of which you can visit four. Filled with faded yet evocative rock art painted with charcoal mixed with manatee fat, the images depict birds, fish and other animals, as well as mysterious human-like figures thought to represent deities. These pictographs are believed to have been painted by the island's pre-Columbus indigenous Taínos, Igneri and Caribs, offering rare insights into ancient Caribbean spirituality and daily life. The principal cave was 'discovered' in 1851 by British explorer Sir Robert Schomburgk, who etched his name on the cave wall.

The caves In addition to the rock art, visitors will find unique geological formations and a cave inhabited by thousands of bats. Conservation efforts are ongoing, as nearby limestone mining continues to threaten the area, casting doubt on any hopes of World Heritage listing.

Guided tours Entry to the park costs RD$100. To enhance your visit, consider hiring a local guide through the **Asociación de Guías Cuevas del Pomier** (fundacioncuevasdelpomier@gmail.com). Contact the president Alex (+1-809-721-5965) on WhatsApp to arrange a bilingual guide. Wear hiking boots and bring a flashlight as the ones on the helmets aren't always great.

Pomier Caves

The Pomier Caves represent the richest historical and cultural treasures in the Caribbean, with more than 6000 pictographs and petroglyphs. It is a complex with more than 55 caves. For the indigenous people of the time, these caves were sacred sanctuaries, places of pilgrimage and spiritual centers. They would shelter here from time to time, and they would come in waves of migration, gathering here to perform daily rituals. These were their sacred churches or temples. In times of rain or hurricanes, the caves served as shelters and, according to Taíno mythology, also as a magical funeral home.

Alex Corporan, *president of the Associación de Guías Cuevas del Pomier*

Listings

BEST OF THE REST

More Southwest Sights

Monumento Natural Dunas de las Calderas

For a majestic Caribbean landscape, visit Baní's fine-sand beachside dunes that rise up to 12m and stretch 15km within a protected reserve. Arrive at sunset for gorgeous views over the water.

OcoaBay

Bet you didn't expect a winery out this way – but welcome to the DR's only vineyard. Set on the coast, this ecofriendly estate revives a 500-year-old tradition with tours and tastings by the sea.

Haitian Market

In the border town of Comendador del Rey this lively Haitian market spills into the streets, with goods such as rum, clothes and produce laid on the ground beneath tarps.

San Juan de la Maguana

Established in 1503, the 'City of Shamans' blends Dominican Catholicism with Haitian Vodou influences, and hosts a religious procession in May featuring possession and spiritual displays.

El Corral de los Indios

Just 5km north of San Juan de la Maguana lies the 'Stonehenge of the Dominican Republic,' a carved pre-Columbian stone in a circular clearing, once used as a ceremonial site for Taínos.

Polo Magnético

In Cabral, 12km west of Barahona, this 'gravity hill' illusion causes cars in neutral to appear to move uphill; a visual trick created by the slope's shape and surrounding landscape.

Barahona Malecón

When exploring the southwest you'll likely transit through Barahona, so head to its waterfront boardwalk for evening food stalls and lively atmosphere.

Bahía de las Águilas Dining

Eco del Mar $$

As well as being one of the DR's most memorable places to stay, with luxury glamping on the sands of Playa Las Cuevas, Eco del Mar offers a fantastic menu of seafood and a beach bar slinging seaside cocktails.

Rancho Tipico $$

One of the southwest's best beach restaurants serves fresh, delicious seafood and some of the best *mofongos* (mashed plantains with meat or seafood) you'll eat. Superb experience across the board.

Restaurante De Bahía Doña Charo $$

Good things come in threes, so here's another lovely seafood option on Playa Las Cuevas, with coconut-flavored fish and grilled lobster to feast on.

GAUTIER STEPHANE/ALAMY

Monumento Natural Dunas de las Calderas

THE SOUTHWEST REVIEWS

Places to Cool Off

Playa Los Patos

Head to the peninsula's northeast coast for this idyllic freshwater swimming hole and scenic pebble beach just south of Paraíso. Things get festive on weekends with Dominican families, but it's quieter midweek.

Playa San Rafael

Another local favorite just southwest of Playa Los Platos, this beautiful palm-fringed beach also has a freshwater lagoon for swimming. Weekends get busy when locals come here for family fun.

Playa Najayo

Just 16km south of San Cristóbal, this popular patch of sand has beach bars offering a taste of local Dominican vibes and flavors.

Playa Palenque

A dip in the ocean in pretty Palenque's vibrant blue waters makes for a refreshing pit stop between Baní and San Cristóbal. Feed on local seafood at its beach shacks.

Las Barias Balneario

The gateway town for Lago Enriquillo, La Descubierta also has a popular freshwater *balneario* (natural swimming hole), Las Barias. It attracts families who come for refreshing dips in its cool spring-fed waters alongside open-air restaurants.

La Toma

A worthwhile stop en route to visiting Reserva Antropológica Cuevas del Pomier, this *balneario* is a wildly popular place for locals to cool off on weekends.

Playa El Cayo

Not exactly pristine, Barahona's city beach makes for a popular outing among locals who relax under the shade of palm trees and enjoy grilled fish, cold beers and dips in the ocean.

DALLAS STRIBLEY/GETTY IMAGES

Playa San Rafael

Playa Pedernales

If you're in town, it's worth dropping by Pedernales' pretty city beach, the DR's most southwesterly patch of sand. Beautiful clear azure waters, wonderful sunsets and peninsula views await.

Playa El Quemaito

Just 14km south of Barahona, Playa El Quemaito is popular for its smooth pebble beach, warm, translucent waters, and beach shacks serving grilled fish and cold beer under thatched-palm umbrellas.

Playa La Caobita

Make the journey 30km southwest of Azua to this fine white-sand beach with crystal-clear waters set among mangroves and places frying up fish.

Playa de Caletón

By no means essential given the amount of beaches along this coastline south of Barahona, but if you've got wheels and are seeking out more isolated beaches, this is another one to check out.

Larimar Jewelry

Escuela Taller y Museo Larimar

In a coastal town 20km south of Barahona, near the world's only Larimar mine, this museum and shop showcases certified Larimar jewelry. Call ahead to watch artisans demonstrate how they craft the stunning pieces.

La Casa del Larimar

Another good spot to pick up beautiful blue Larimar pieces, this certified shop centrally located in Barahona has very knowledgeable staff who will be able to field all your questions about this rare stone if you're not able to make it to the mines.

Yamir Larimar Jewelry

On the outskirts of Barahona south of the center, this boutique store specializes in the rare blue silicate pectolite stone, sold as individual pieces or crafted into jewelry.

Tienda y Taller de Larimar Vanessa

Just 1km south of Escuela Taller y Museo Larimar,this family-owned Larimar workshop sells beautiful aquamarine Larimar earrings, pendants and keepsakes.

Coastal Eats

La Esquinita De Kelvin Sandwich $

Putting in a strong case for the region's best sandwich, this popular lunch stop in Baní has a long list of carb-loaded goodness that expands to burgers and tacos. Go the meat-filled *completo especial*.

Pasteleria Chichita $

This place has been serving San Cristóbal's signature pastel *en hoja* ('pastry in paper') for over 50 years. The chicken and yucca version, naturally in a paper bag, is especially tasty.

El Meson Suizo $$

One of the southwest's better dining spots, this stylish Ázua restaurant serves delicious *mofongos*, grilled meats and seafood on its atmospheric outdoor patio.

Caney Beach Home $$

For another option in Baní, head to the sands of Playa Matanzas for this luxurious glamping accommodations serving delicious, exotic Caribbean dishes (think seafood-filled pineapples), paella and coconut mojitos.

Rincón Mexicano $$

Lovers of Mexican food may be tempted to come by San Juan de la Maguana just for the authentic tacos (RD$110) alone, or at the very least its margaritas!

Restaurant La Galeria del Espía $$

Another option for San Juan de la Maguana, just across from Parque Central, this popular spot makes quick, tasty Dominican food. It has a plate of the day, along with an alternating menu of fresh, traditional food.

Mojito Bar y Restaurante $$

An enticing beachfront restaurant in Playa La Cienaga, just south of the Escuela Taller y Museo Larimar, with sparkling views and lavish, fresh seafood feasts.

El Corral de los Indios (p226)

Restaurant King Crab $$

Just a short jaunt from Playa Pedernales, west of the Malecón, this long-time favorite for fresh fish, seafood, lobster and crab specialties has a pleasant terrace setting.

Restaurante Ibiza $$

Also in Pedernale is this local fave for Dominican fare, including all manner of fish and seafood (crab, shrimp, conch), and a few pasta and meat options.

El Navio Bar and Seafood $$

Beachfront deck dining and tasty seafood, meats and Dominican snacks are enjoyed alongside dreamy Caribbean views.

Restaurante La Matica $$

Directly south of San Cristóbal, live the Caribbean dream by treating yourself to heavenly fried fish and lobster.

Le Nua Bistro Bar $$

A classy San Cristóbal option offering creative, contemporary culinary cuisine.

Baya Onda $$$

Part of OcoaBay vineyard, this quality estate restaurant with a farm-to-table ethos serves locally sourced produce from goat cheese to honey, alongside wood-fired focaccia and seafood dishes.

Barahona Eating

The Breaking $

'Food and beer' is the tagline here, and boy, does it deliver. Awesome artisanal burgers (including a triple smash), wings and Dominican barbecue are washed down with craft beers and original cocktails.

DALLAS STRIBLEY/GETTY IMAGES

Playa San Rafael (p227)

Cafetería La Esquina De Fidel $

Famous for its sandwiches, Fidel Cafe Corner is a Barahona institution: a no-frills corner shack eatery doing loaded toasted panini.

Restaurante Foodtopia $

Open-air food park with a choice of anything from *mofongos*, pizza, burgers and Mexican to go with beers and cocktails.

Brisas del Caribe $$

A well-regarded restaurant with a waterfront terrace serving a menu of flavorsome, freshly caught seafood including lobster, shrimp and kingfish.

Restaurante Delicias Marinas $$

Near the Malecón, this seafood specialty restaurant has a delicious selection of broths, stews and lobster dishes.

Practicalities

EASY STEPS FROM THE AIRPORT TO THE CITY CENTERS

For a relatively small country, the Dominican Republic sure has a lot of international airports – seven at last count. The busiest are Punta Cana (pictured below), Santo Domingo, Puerto Plata and Santiago. Where you fly into depends on your interests, but consider flying into one city and out of another to mix things up and explore more of the country.

AT THE AIRPORT

SIM CARDS
Cell phone providers Claro, Altice and Viva have prepaid SIM cards. You can buy Claro and Altice SIM cards at Santo Domingo Airport; otherwise, it's easy to get one in major towns (bring your passport). Another option is to purchase an eSIM compatible with local networks before you leave.

CURRENCY EXCHANGE
Currency exchange offices are available at most international airports, but rates are much better in town. US dollars are widely accepted, so bring enough to tide you over until you find better rates in town. Have a few dollar bills for tips.

MULEVICH/SHUTTERSTOCK

WI-FI Free wi-fi is available at major international airports with good coverage throughout their terminals.

ATMS Banco Popular, Banco BHD León, Banco Progreso and Scotiabank accept foreign cards. ATM fees are pricey and maximum withdrawal amounts limited.

CHARGING STATIONS Most airports will have dedicated charge stations to juice up devices; otherwise, a power bank is a fail-proof backup.

EXPORT RESTRICTIONS

No cigar Cigar lovers can run into trouble when bringing cigars back into their own countries, with maximum export restrictions being 100 for the US and 50 for Canada and most European nations; Australia even less. So don't stock up.

Gems Exporting raw, unpolished amber from the DR is illegal, so only purchase polished certified amber jewelry and other pieces.

GETTING TO THE CITY CENTERS

Bus There's no direct bus from Aeropuerto Internacional Las Américas to Santo Domingo, though routes from Aeropuerto Internacional Punta Cana to Punta Cana exist with extra transfers. From Aeropuerto Internacional Gregorio Luperón in Puerto Plata, walk 500m to the highway to catch a *guagua*.

Rideshare Uber operates at Santo Domingo, Punta Cana and Santiago airports, but not Puerto Plata. Availability changes and short walks may be required.

Taxi Always available; fares range from US$20 to US$50. No meters, so negotiate beforehand.

HOW MUCH FOR A...

Bus
US$10
One hour

Rideshare
US$25
30 minutes

Taxi
US$20–50
30 minutes

Car Rental If you're planning to explore widely, renting a car from the airport offers the most flexibility.

Hotel Shuttle Many travelers rely on transport arranged by their hotel – an easy, stress-free option that ensures peace of mind.

Are you experienced? One important factor when considering car rental is road safety (p234) – especially after a long flight and the challenge of navigating busy city traffic. So unless you're seasoned to the conditions, renting a car may be better suited for relaxed rural side trips rather than driving in hectic urban areas like Santo Domingo.

OTHER POINTS OF ENTRY

Cruise ships A popular stop on Caribbean cruise itineraries, the DR sees many international cruise ships dock at locations across the island. Most stop at Santo Domingo, Isla Catalina near La Romana (part of Casa de Campo), Cayo Levantado in the Península de Samaná, and Amber Cove just outside Puerto Plata up north. All the above ports allow passengers to disembark for excursions on land.

Haiti Though at the time of research borders were closed, there are four official land border crossings between the DR and Haiti. Political tensions have occasionally disrupted movement, so check current conditions before traveling. Ordinarily, the most popular crossings include: Jimaní–Malpasse, linking Santo Domingo with Port-au-Prince, this is the busiest and best-organized crossing. Dajabón–Ouanaminthe, a busy northern route, links Santiago and Cap-Haïtien; avoid busy Mondays and Fridays due to market crowds. Pedernales–Anse-à-Pitres is a remote southern bridge crossing.

Puerto Rico Ferries del Caribe (ferriesdelcaribe.com) operates a ferry service between Santo Domingo and San Juan. It departs three times a week and takes about 14 hours.

TRANSPORTATION TIPS TO HELP YOU GET AROUND

Traveling in the Dominican Republic is quite manageable in terms of distances. Whether driving or taking public transportation, its most popular destinations are within three to four hours of each other. However, in more remote, mountainous regions, roads are tougher going and require the use of a 4WD; otherwise, consider booking some tours.

BUS

The DR has a great, affordable bus system, with comfortable, air-con, 1st-class buses with toilets offering frequent services between major towns. Caribe Tours (caribetours.com.do), Expreso Bávaro (expresobavaro.com) and Metro (metroserviciosturisticos.com) are the main companies.

CAR

Though public transportation will serve your needs, having your own car is the most convenient way to explore the DR. If not for the entire trip, consider renting one for a few days for day trips to rural areas. Be prepared for tough driving conditions and reckless drivers.

4WD rental per day from US$130

Petrol approx RD$240/gallon

Local *guagua* RD$35–70

ROAD CONDITIONS Not for the faint-hearted, roads in the DR can vary wildly from excellent to terrible within just a few kilometers. Hence driving is a challenge even for experienced drivers – a hazardous mix of potholes, speeding cars, swerving motorcycles and overloaded vehicles. Be particularly careful at night. Better yet, never drive at night; it's especially risky with poorly lit roads and drink-driving posing extra dangers.

CAR RENTAL Car-rental agencies are at major airports and cities. Choose larger companies for better vehicles, reliable service and comprehensive insurance. Rates are cheaper online. For more rural regions, a 4WD is recommended.

GUAGUA *Guaguas*, small local buses or minivans, are common. They hold around 25 passengers and can be flagged down on the side of the road in the direction you're heading. Most pass every 15 to 30 minutes and cost RD$35 to RD$70.

DRIVING ESSENTIALS

Most travelers can use their home driver's license.

Drive on the right; steering wheel is on the left.

Gas stations are common; keep your tank at least half full.

40km/h in cities; 80km/h outside cities; 120km/h on highways.

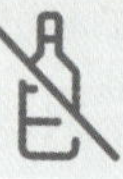

The legal blood alcohol limit is 0.05%.

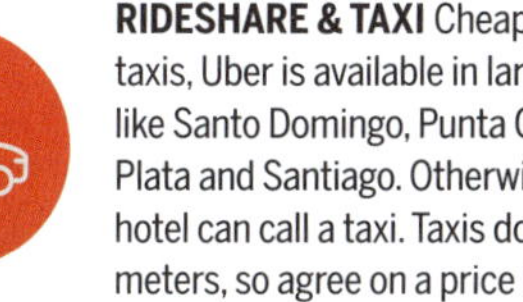

RIDESHARE & TAXI Cheaper than taxis, Uber is available in larger towns like Santo Domingo, Punta Cana, Puerto Plata and Santiago. Otherwise, your hotel can call a taxi. Taxis don't use meters, so agree on a price beforehand.

LOCAL TRANSPORTATION For shorter trips, *motoconchos* (motorcycle taxis) are cheap, with an average fare of RD$30, and are often the only option. Always negotiate prices, insist on a helmet and ask the driver to slow down *(¡Más despacio por favor!)*. Another affordable option is Públicos (shared minivans or cars), costing around RD$15. If you're the only passenger, confirm you're paying the public fare to avoid higher private 'taxi' rates.

BICYCLE Though the DR's highways aren't ideal for cycling, its rural back roads and lesser-used highways are perfect for mountain biking. Tour companies in Jarabacoa and Cabarete offer biking experiences. For multiday rides, consider bringing your own bike.

KNOW YOUR CARBON FOOTPRINT A one-way flight from Santo Domingo to Puerto Plata would emit about 64kg of carbon dioxide per passenger. A car would emit 36kg, while a bus would emit 1.4kg for the same distance, per passenger.

ROAD DISTANCE CHART (KMS)

	Santo Domingo	Punta Cana	Samaná	Las Terrenas	Santiago	Jarabacoa	Puerto Plata	Cabarete	Barahona	Pedernales
Punta Cana	195									
Samaná	180	325								
Las Terrenas	160	300	40							
Santiago	160	355	205	185						
Jarabacoa	155	340	185	160	55					
Puerto Plata	215	405	215	190	70	105				
Cabarete	210	400	175	155	75	100	40			
Barahona	180	375	360	340	320	310	375	370		
Pedernales	305	495	470	460	440	315	495	490	115	
Bayahibe	145	65	270	250	300	290	355	350	340	440

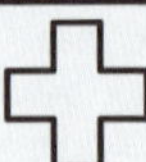

SAFE TRAVEL

The Dominican Republic is generally a safe destination. In larger towns, be sure to follow the usual 'big city' precautions – do not flaunt valuables and take care of your phone. Be mindful of road safety, rough swimming conditions and food health too.

GET HOME SAFE In cities, avoid walking at night, particularly after 10pm if you've been drinking at bars and clubs. Also steer clear of beaches after dark. Instead, take an Uber or a taxi home or to your next destination.

DON'T DRINK THE WATER Use purified water for drinking and brushing your teeth. Avoid accidentally swallowing water in the shower, too. Contaminated food or water can cause serious illness – bring electrolytes to rehydrate, and seek medical help if symptoms occur. Top tip: carry hand sanitizer to ensure good hygiene.

NIGHT DRIVING Poor lighting and an array of road hazards (particularly drunk, speeding motorists) makes night driving downright dangerous. It's probably best avoided altogether, so plan ahead to leave enough time to reach your destination before nightfall, or take a taxi if traveling locally.

SWIMMING SAFETY Many beaches have a killer combo of strong surf and riptides. Swim with caution (or avoid going in beyond your waist) and never fight a riptide – swim parallel to the shore until you're free, then head in.

FILIPPO CARLOT/SHUTTERSTOCK

THEFT Avoid talking on or looking at cell phones in public (thieves are known to snatch them). Car theft is not unheard of, so don't leave valuables inside your car.

BORDER CROSSINGS

Though closed at the time of research for travelers, tensions along the Haitian border flare up occasionally; check the situation with your country's travel advisory website before crossing.

HURRICANES

Hurricanes occasionally hit the DR in July and August. Monitor local news or the US National Hurricane Center (nhc.noaa.gov). Follow evacuation advice, stock up on supplies, and avoid beaches, rivers and flood-prone areas.

QUICK TIPS TO HELP YOU MANAGE YOUR MONEY

CREDIT CARDS Credit and debit cards are widely accepted across the areas most frequented by tourists. With that said, many places, especially in rural regions, accept only cash. Businesses may add a 16% surcharge to card payments. Always check your bill before signing, as overcharging on credit card transactions has been reported.

ATMS
ATMs are common but have low withdrawal limits (up to RD$20,000). For larger amounts, withdraw inside banks with your passport.

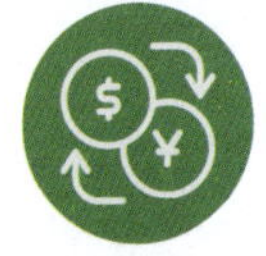

MONEY CHANGERS
Money changers may approach you, but are best avoided. Stick to ATMs, banks or *cambios* (exchange offices).

CASH

The Dominican peso (RD$) is the official currency, divided into 100 centavos (cents), though prices are usually rounded to the nearest peso. Coins include RD$1 and RD$5, while notes range from RD$10 to RD$2000. In tourist areas, US dollars are often accepted, and tour operators often quote prices in US dollars but accept pesos at the current exchange rate.

CURRENCY

Dominican peso (RD$)

HOW MUCH FOR A...

500mL beer
RD$150

Snorkeling trip
RD$2000

Beachside meal
RD$500–880

DOUBLE COUNT Though in many cases it's a legitimate error in math, travelers have reported being shortchanged, so it pays to double-check the bill.

BARGAINING
When buying souvenirs, jewelry or artwork it's not uncommon to bargain. Most vendors are friendly and relaxed, and can offer a bit of wiggle room even if there's a price tag.

BUDGET TIPS
The best approach for budget travelers is to live like a local as opposed to a tourist – take public transportation, eat local and stay in locally run guesthouses.

TIPPING Tipping in the DR is often added to the bill, with restaurants adding 28% (18% tax and 10% service charge). With that said, if service is exceptional, always leave more. In hotels, a US$1 tip per night for housekeeping is appreciated; round up for taxis; and tour guides should be tipped US$5 to US$10 for full-day excursions. Bring small US bills, as they're widely accepted and useful for tips, especially in resorts.

POSITIVE-IMPACT TRAVEL

ON THE ROAD

Eco-resorts All-inclusive luxury resorts are popular, but come with significant environmental costs, including waste, water overuse and energy consumption. Opt for ecolodges or resorts that follow clear sustainability practices, support local communities and reduce their ecological footprint. Choosing wisely can make a big difference.

Ecotourism For activities like trekking, diving and wildlife-watching, seek out certified sustainable operators or grassroots initiatives that prioritize environmental care and community involvement.

Take the bus The DR is working toward sustainable transportation but hasn't fully transitioned yet. To reduce emissions and fuel use, buses or shared vehicles are a more ecofriendly choice than private cars and domestic flights.

Leave no trace Remote beaches and parks lack bins so take all rubbish with you.

Pedal power Explore the Central Highlands villages by mountain bike for a low-impact adventure.

TOMAS KONOPASEK/SHUTTERSTOCK

GIVE BACK

Many NGOs in the DR are community-based organizations focused on developing sustainable ecotourism. While formal volunteering programs can be limited, Spanish-speaking travelers with specific skills can offer meaningful ways to contribute. Always research thoroughly to assess the credibility and understand the goals of any organization before committing.

CEDAF (cedaf.org.do) Nationwide NGO helping local farmers develop sustainable land-use practices.

Grupo Jaragua (grupojaragua.org.do) Well-respected, long-established NGO active in DR's southwest supporting biodiversity and community livelihoods through initiatives from guiding to beekeeping.

Punta Cana Ecological Foundation (puntacana.org) One of DR's pioneers in sustainable development, it runs projects focused on coral reef restoration and environmental protection.

DOS & DON'TS

Do be patient. Dominican culture is polite, relaxed and unhurried.

Do avoid wearing beachwear in towns, shops or restaurants.

Do learn a few basic greetings and slang in Spanish to show respect and connect with locals.

Don't shout to get attention – hissing is the accepted and polite way to do this.

LEAVE A SMALL FOOTPRINT

Calculate your carbon There are a number of online calculators. Try resurgence.org/resources/carbon-calculator.html.

Avoid single-use plastics Reusable shopping bags, cups and cutlery make a ecofriendly travel kit that helps reduce plastics that can be harmful to marine life.

Be mindful of conservation Take shorter showers, conserve water while brushing your teeth and avoid wasting water. Don't change towels regularly. When leaving rooms, turn off the air-conditioning to reduce energy consumption.

EDUCATION IMAGES/GETTY IMAGES

SUPPORT LOCAL

Few experiences are more quintessentially Dominican than sipping Presidente *grandes* outside a *colmado* (grocery store) or enjoying a *plato del día* (plate of the day) at a local *comedor* (budget restaurant). Even if you're staying at an all-inclusive, check these out and give locals a fair share of the tourism income. For the most authentic experiences, get out into the countryside and seek out local guides, family-run guesthouses and handmade crafts.

CLIMATE CHANGE & TRAVEL

Lonely Planet urges all travelers to engage with their travel carbon footprint, which will mainly come from air travel. While there often isn't an alternative, travelers can look to minimize the number of flights they take, opt for newer aircrafts and use cleaner ground transportation, such as trains.

One proposed solution—purchasing carbon offsets—unfortunately does not cancel out the impact of individual flights. While most destinations will depend on air travel for the foreseeable future, for now, pursuing ground-based travel where possible is the best course of action.

The UN Carbon Offset Calculator shows how flying impacts a household's emissions:

The ICAO's carbon emissions calculator allows visitors to analyse the CO^2 generated by point-to-point journeys:

RESOURCES

puntacana.org

grupojaragua.org.do

cedaf.org.do

godominicanrepublic.com

UNIQUE AND LOCAL WAYS TO STAY

The DR has a wide variety of accommodations catering to all tastes and budgets. From sprawling all-inclusive mega resorts, boutique hotels and family-run pensions to lively backpackers, surf camps and tree house ecolodges, you will find plenty of unique experiences to choose from across the island.

HOW MUCH FOR A...

Dorm bed
US$20

Boutique hostel
US$100–350

All-inclusive
US$200–500

MAURITIUS IMAGES GMBH/ALAMY

BUDGET STAYS Better known for resorts than hostels, the DR still has plenty of independently owned, family-run budget guesthouses and backpacker hangouts. Spots like Island Life Hostel (islandlifehostel.com) and La Choza in Santo Domingo, Hostel 23 in Las Terrenas, and Cabarete Surf Camp (p143) are great for meeting fellow travelers and sharing stories.

Outdoor lovers will find free cabins on the Pico Duarte trail (p174), while Spirit Mountain (p195) hires campsites with tents. For glamping, Eco del Mar (ecodelmar.com.do) features affordable beachside tents that unzip to stunning sea views.

ECOLODGES

From riverside lodges to mountaintop retreats, the DR offers enchanting ecolodges that connect guests with rural life. Sleep in treetop bungalows at the *Avatar*-like Dominican Tree House Village (p114) or Spirit Mountain's organic coffee farm (p171). For sweeping views and community-based tourism, try Tubagua Ecolodge (pictured above; p154).

SURF ACCOMMODATIONS Whether you're here to carve up waves, catch the wind, dive underwater or tick off birds, the DR offers dedicated accommodations for many popular outdoor activities. Cabarete and the North Coast have bohemian kiteboarding and surf camps; elsewhere, you'll find dive resorts and bird-watching lodges.

MIRJANA SIMEUNOVICH/SHUTTERSTOCK

WATERFRAME/SHUTTERSTOCK

ALL-INCLUSIVE RESORTS If you're looking for a quintessential hassle-free holiday, a stay at an all-inclusive resort makes a lot of sense. These resorts offer relatively luxurious beachfront stays at great value, with a single price typically covering accommodations, food, drinks and a variety of activities – plus access to pools, gyms and exclusive beach areas.

The highest concentration of resorts is in Bávaro and Punta Cana, the DR's most popular tourist destination. Other resort areas include Playa Dorada on the North Coast (pictured left), known for good-value packages; Las Terrenas, which blends beach life with a charming European vibe and outdoor adventure; and Juan Dolio and Boca Chica – both within striking distance of Santo Domingo. For something smaller and more low-key, try Playa Dominicus near Bayahibe.

It's crucial to do your research and consider the following: is the resort beachfront? What is included? Is it family-friendly or adults-only? What entertainment is available?

One common complaint is the poor quality of buffet food. Sticking to the resort often means missing out on local dining and cultural experiences. Many resorts offer day passes ranging from US$50 to US$150.

BOOKING Booking online usually delivers the lowest rates. Reserving in advance is advised during the high season, which runs from December to February – the perfect storm of Christmas holidays, ideal beach weather, big surf and Carnival celebrations. Regardless of the time of year, all-inclusive resorts should always be booked ahead. For the best deals, compare online prices with those from a travel agent in your home country.

Colonial Tours (colonialtours.com) Bookings and price comparisons on all-inclusive resorts.

Lonely Planet (lonelyplanet.com/hotels) Trusted, independent reviews and booking links.

Booking.com Provides a vast range of options, along with user reviews and free cancellation policies.

Airbnb (airbnb.com) Great for independent travelers, but stick to well-reviewed listings.

HostelWorld (hostelworld.com) Caters specifically to backpackers and includes user feedback on dorms and budget stays.

Go Dominican Republic (godominicanrepublic.com/places-to-stay) Doesn't handle bookings, but the extensive accommodations listings are a useful reference.

JANE SWEENEY/ALAMY

HISTORIC STAYS In older cities, you'll find boutique hotels like Casas del XVI (casasdelxvi.com) and Nicolás de Ovando (hodelpa.com/nicolas-de-ovando; pictured above) in restored colonial buildings oozing character, history and luxury.

ESSENTIAL NUTS & BOLTS

VISA

Most visitors don't need to apply for a visa before arrival: tourist cards are now included in airfares, allowing stays of up to 30 days.

SMOKING

Permitted in public spaces – including indoors – except at medical facilities and schools. Most resorts, however, enforce a different set of rules.

TOILETS

There are restrooms in most public buildings. Dispose of toilet paper in a waste basket to avoid blockage.

FAST FACTS

Time Zone
GMT-4 (EST)

Country Code
+1

Electricity
120V/
60Hz

GOOD TO KNOW

The US$10 fee for tourist cards is now included in all airfares.

The DR uses the metric system for everything except gasoline, which is measured in gallons, and at laundromats, where laundry is measured in pounds.

In case of emergency dial 911; for fire 112.

The legal drinking age in the DR is 18.

Spanish is DR's official language, but English is widely spoken in the tourism industry.

ACCESSIBLE TRAVEL

General accessibility Infrastructure in public areas and attractions can be inconsistent or lacking. However, attitudes are welcoming – Dominicans are resourceful and quick to offer assistance.

Resorts The best option for travelers with mobility impairments. Some resorts offer wheelchair-accessible rooms with wide doors and accessible bathrooms.

Cruises Taking a cruise is one of the easiest ways to explore the Caribbean, providing a convenient entry point.

Public spaces & transportation Accessibility on public transportation is limited; sidewalks and buildings often lack ramps or lifts.

Useful resources Asociación Dominicana de Rehabilitación (adr.org.do), Fundación Dominicana de Ciegos (fundociegos.org.do).

TOURIST INFORMATION

Most tourist towns have info stands with maps, schedules and tips. Visit godominicanrepublic.com.

LGBTQI+ ONLINE RESOURCES

visitdominicanrepublic.com/up-close/essential-lgbtq-travel-guide-dominican-republic

WI-FI

Widely available in cafes, restaurants and hotels; coverage can be patchy in remote, rural areas.

FAMILY TRAVEL

Resorts All-inclusive resorts are especially convenient for families, offering meals, kid-friendly activities and pools.

Breastfeeding Uncommon in public, so discretion is advised.

Supplies Major grocery stores carry diapers and baby food.

Entry fees Many museums and cultural attractions have free or half-price admission for children under 12 or 13.

Safety Child safety seats aren't common; consider bringing your own. Most resorts have high chairs.

IMPORTS & EXPORTS

Visitors may bring in limited alcohol and tobacco; prescriptions are advised for medications. Exporting antiques, raw amber or endangered species products is illegal. Cigar limits often cause issues with customs.

OPENING HOURS

Opening hours vary by season and location but generally banks open 8:30am to 5pm weekdays and 9am to 1pm Saturdays; shops and supermarkets open 8am to 10pm Monday to Saturday; restaurants 8am to 10pm; and government offices run 9am to 2:30pm weekdays. Bars open late and museums follow their own schedules.

BENNIAN/SHUTTERSTOCK

LGBTIQ+ TRAVELERS

Though it remains a predominantly conservative, Catholic society, attitudes are slowly shifting. However, prejudices remain regarding same-sex relationships and discrimination against the LGBTIQ+ community is fairly widespread.

Public displays of affection are frowned upon, but same-sex couples usually won't face issues booking hotel rooms or enjoying their stay discreetly.

Diversidad Dominicana (diversidaddominicana.org) is a nonprofit organization based in Santo Domingo that does great work in campaigning for LGBTIQ+ rights.

PHRASES TO GET YOU TALKING

Spanish pronunciation is easy, as most sounds have equivalents in English. Also, Spanish spelling is phonetically consistent, meaning that there's a clear and consistent relationship between what you see in writing and how it's pronounced.

If you read our pronunciation guides as if they were English, you'll be understood. Note that *kh* is a throaty sound (like the '*ch*' in the Scottish loch), *v* and *b* are like a soft English '*v*' (between a '*v*' and a '*b*'), and *r* is strongly rolled. The stressed syllables are in italics in our pronunciation guides.

BASICS

Hello.	*Hola.*	*o*·la
Goodbye.	*Adiós.*	a·*dyos*
Yes.	*Sí.*	see
No.	*No.*	no
Please.	*Por favor.*	por fa·*vor*
Thank you.	*Gracias.*	*gra*·syas
Excuse me.	*Con permiso.*	kon per·*mee*·so
Sorry.	*Perdón.*	per·*don*

What's your name?
¿Cómo se llama usted? — *ko*·mo se *ya*·ma oo·*sted* (polite)
¿Cómo te llamas? — *ko*·mo te *ya*·mas (informal)

My name is ...
Me llamo ... — me *ya*·mo ...

Do you speak English?
¿Habla inglés? — *a*·bla een·*gles* (polite)
¿Hablas inglés? — *a*·blas een·*gles* (informal)

I don't understand.
Yo no entiendo. — yo no en·*tyen*·do

TIME & NUMBERS

What time is it?	*¿Qué hora es?*	ke *o*·ra es
It's (10) o'clock.	*Son (las diez).*	son (las dyes)
Half past (1).	*Es (la una) y media.*	es (la *oo*·na) ee *me*·dya
morning	*mañana*	ma·*nya*·na
afternoon	*tarde*	*tar*·de
evening	*noche*	*no*·che
yesterday	*ayer*	a·*yer*
today	*hoy*	oy
tomorrow	*mañana*	ma·*nya*·na

1	*uno*	*oo*·no	**6**	*seis*	seys
2	*dos*	dos	**7**	*siete*	*sye*·te
3	*tres*	tres	**8**	*ocho*	*o*·cho
4	*cuatro*	*kwa*·tro	**9**	*nueve*	*nwe*·ve
5	*cinco*	*seen*·ko	**10**	*diez*	dyes

EMERGENCIES

Help!	*¡Socorro!*	so·*ko*·ro
Go away!	*¡Váyase!*	*va*·ya·se
Call a ...!	*¡Llame a ...!*	*ya*·me a...
the police	*la policía*	la po·lee·*see*·a
a doctor	*un doctor*	oon dok·*tor*
I'm lost.	*Estoy perdido/a.*	es·*toy* per·*dee*·do/a (m/f)

Index

000 Map pages

000 Map pages

'The names and biographies of the historical figures who lived, worked and fought in Santo Domingo's Zona Colonial are a veritable who's who of seminal figures from the early 16th-century 'age of contact.' Walking through the neighborhood's colonial-era streets and homes, brings this otherwise distant historical period to life in ways no textbook ever could.'

MICHAEL GROSBERG

'If life's a beach, then gazing at Cabarete's dreamy sea with lobster and cold beer in hand is truly living!'

TRENT HOLDEN

GIUSEPPECRIMENI/SHUTTERSTOCK, CHRISTOPHER V JONES/SHUTTERSTOCK

THIS BOOK

Destination editor
Akanksha Singh

Product editor
Lauren O'Connell

Cartographer
Julie Dodkins

Book designer
Jo-anne Riddell

Assisting editor
Anne Mulvaney

Cover researcher
Giada de Agostinis

Thanks Ronan Abayawickrema, James Appleton, Michelle Bennett, Gwen Cotter, Melanie Dankel, John Taufa, Darren O'Connell, Saralinda Turner